Finish the Script!

This book is a work of fiction. Any reference to historical events, real people, or real locals are used factiously. Other names, characters, places, and incidents are the product of the author's imagination, and any resemblance to actual events or locales or persons, living or dead, is entirely coincidental.

Finish The Script!
Published by Majestic Arts

Cover design by Scott King
Edited by Angela Gouletas

Manufactured in the United States of America

Library of Congress Cataloging-in-Publication Data

King, Scott
Finish The Script!
P. CM.

Copyright ©2013 Scott King

ISBN-10: 1492820865
ISBN-13: 978-1492820864

All rights reserved. No part of this book may be reproduced in any form or by any means without permission in writing from the author, except for the inclusion of brief quotations in a review.

Attention all readers! The author, publisher, and all those involved wish it to be made clear that dealing with fictional characters can be addicting. Becoming a writer will not fix your real world problems, but if you are lucky you may find some a new sense of satisfaction.

Books By Scott King:

Holiday Wars
Holiday Wars Volume 1: The Holiday Spirit
Holiday Wars Volume 2: Winter's Wrath
Holiday Wars Volume 3: Queen's Gambit

Zimmah Chronicles
Cupcakes vs. Brownies
Mermaids vs. Unicorns*

DAD! A Documentary Graphic Novel
National Cthulhu Eats Spaghetti Day*

*Forthcoming

CONTENTS

1.	*Finding the Idea*	*10*
2.	*Writing the Elevator Pitch*	*18*
3.	*Character Creation*	*29*
4.	*Character Arcs*	*43*
5.	*Writing the Treatment*	*53*
6.	*The Beat Sheet*	*61*
7.	*Figuring Out the Details*	*76*
8.	*Scene Outline*	*84*
9.	*Software and Format*	*90*
10.	*Writing Prose*	*94*
11.	*Writing Dialogue*	*99*
12.	*What's in a Scene?*	*108*
13.	*Making Time*	*112*
14.	*Getting Through Act I*	*116*
15.	*Getting Through Act II*	*142*
16.	*Getting Through Act III*	*155*
17.	*Rewriting*	*163*
18.	*Now What?*	*183*

Finish the Script!
A College Screenwriting Course In Book Form

Scott King

Introduction

Hey, you.

So here we are, you and I. In many ways, this is like a first date. We are getting together in a common place, the Introduction, and we are both judging each other, trying to figure each other out.

SNARFLAX!

You see that? That was your fault. Because I knew you were judging me, I got all self-conscious and felt the desire to show off. So maybe it would be best if we both go into this by being honest and putting all our cards on the table. That sound good?

There is only one thing I'm hoping to get from this relationship... no, not that! What's wrong with you? This is a PG-rated book. Get your mind out of the gutter. Geez.

I want to help you. That's it.

I went through the system growing up — the educational system. It was really bumpy at times. In both undergraduate and grad school, I had classes that were a complete bust. There were full semesters when I asked myself, "This is what I'm paying for?" But along the way there were a few special classes with the most amazing professors. I met people who literally helped shape who I've become as an artist and a creator. And that's what I want to do for you on your journey to becoming a writer. I want to open doors and help you see stories in ways you never have.

If that sounds OK with you, then let's get started.

How to Use This Book

The number one thing I say to my students is "Finish the Script." It sounds so simple, but it's not. It takes a lot of patience and a lot of willpower to finish a first draft, and then it takes even more to go back and do a rewrite. If you actually finish that rewrite, you will easily be ahead of the other 97% of people who are just wanna-be writers. So if you ever get stuck throughout this whole process, just imagine me screaming in your ear, "FINISH THE SCRIPT!" If for some reason you're imagination challenged (which would be weird because clearly you want to learn how to be a writer, which automatically implies that you have a vivid imagination) then fake it.

In many ways, this book is set up just like my college writing class. Most chapters start with an introduction that is often anecdotal or silly. Normally, when I start class, I tell a funny story about my latest exploits and adventures. It's a good icebreaker that gets everyone warmed up and paying attention for the day. That's when I jump in with the lecture. Sometimes they are short, and sometimes they are really long. I've always let the subject matter dictate the length. When I'm done with the lecture, I give my students an assignment, and it's up to them to get it done. The chapters in this book will work the same way.

The one thing I want you to keep in mind throughout this whole journey is that there are no real rules when it comes to writing. Writing is a personal thing. A process that works for one person may not work for someone else. A perfect example is that I'm a morning person. I wake up early, and I'm sharper and more focused in the first few hours of the day than at any other time. As a result, it's best for me to do my writing in the morning. The flip side is that I know tons of fabulous writers who stay up really late and do all their real writing between 11 p.m. and 4 a.m. Writing in the morning doesn't make me better than people who write at night, because there is no right or wrong. There is only what works best for you.

I'm going to throw a lot of different lectures and assignments at you, because one of the first steps to becoming a writer is learning what works for you. Sometimes the assignments are going to click and make perfect sense, and sometimes they will feel like a real chore. That's OK. That's how it's supposed to be. Just suck it up, get it done and finish the script!

Keep in mind too that this isn't a book on how to break into the business, and I'm telling you upfront that no one learned how to write a screenplay solely from a book. Scriptwriting books don't replace the act of scriptwriting. My goal here is to start you on the learning process, and just like any kind of writing, most of your success will depend on you. You have to be willing to put in the time and be open minded. You have to have the determination to finish it, because me writing "Finish the Script!" will get you only so far without you doing the work you need to do. But that's OK, because I believe in you.

CHAPTER ONE

Finding the idea

The first movie I worked on was "Runaway Bride." I was in high school and I got the job by manipulating myself into it. I was working on the high school newspaper, and when we heard that a big-studio movie was going to film in our small town, I knew right away that I wanted to write the article about it. Our advisor didn't think that was a good idea, since she considered me a "weird duck" and didn't want me embarrassing the school. I didn't let that stop me.

My family owned a restaurant in Berlin, Md., where the movie was filmed. That meant that when the town council had a session with business owners to vote on whether to allow the movie to be filmed in Berlin, I got myself into that meeting — and the reporter from our school paper assigned to the story was nowhere to be seen. Director Gary Marshall was at the meeting, as were his assistant director and locations manager. There was a ton of local press, both TV and newspaper.

After the council meeting, the town opened up the floor for questions. Every single business owner was quiet because they were seeing dollar signs. The local press spoke out, but it was silly stuff. "Who's going to be in the movie?" "How big is the budget?" and other generic questions. When I stood up, I cut right to the heart of the matter and said, "How long will local businesses have to be shut down for production, and how will street closures affect residents and school bus routes?" Yeah, I was brat back then.

What's crazy though is that the locations manager called my high school the next day and talked to my principals. Later that day, I was called to the office, and my principal said I was offered a job on the movie. Of course I took it, and it was one of the most educational experiences of my life. Without having worked on the movie, I don't know if I would've ever had the guts to go to school with the intention of getting a film degree.

The lesson here isn't, "Oh, look at me, I'm so cool because I worked on a random romantic comedy movie when I was in high school in the '90s." The point is that if I hadn't taken the initiative and snuck my way into that town council meeting, my whole life would probably be very different right now. And it's that kind of risk I want you guys to be taking with your writing. Take chances. Be brave. We learn just as much from mistakes as successes, and I don't want you guys holding back.

Where Do You Get Ideas?

I attend comic book conventions and book signings, often with other guests. Recently at a bookstore signing, a woman asked the author I was signing with where she gets her ideas. The author responded with, "From the Idea of the Month Club." I think she meant it as a joke, but it came off really snarky. After the woman walked away, the author turned to me and said, "I hate when people ask that."

Writers hate that question because there is no real answer. Ideas can be inspired by many different things, but at the end of the day, an idea is simply born in a writer's head. Speaking personally, my own ideas just come to me. There is no rhyme or reason as to when or why. There are tools and methods I can use to make them come faster, but in general, I have very little control over them at all. So if you are having trouble trying to come up with an idea for what to write about, it's best to look at yourself. No one can magically create an idea for you.

Because everyone gets ideas from different places, there is no right or wrong way to come up with them. It's really about whatever works for you. In my case, I like to bombard myself with storytelling as if it were gamma radiation and I were Bruce Banner. I watch nearly every major scripted show on all broadcast and big cable networks. I devour novels like glasses of water. I watch almost every movie that gets a theatrical release, and I read both floppy comics and graphic novels. For me, as a writer, it's important to know what else is out there. Plus, by being exposed to so much, I am more easily inspired.

But it's often not the good stuff that inspires me. Normally, if I'm watching or reading something really good, I'll be so sucked into the story that my mind won't have time to brainstorm or otherwise run off to do its own thing. It's the bad movies and poor-quality writing that cause my brain to go into overdrive, because instead of enjoying the story, I'll say to myself, "Oh, they really screwed this up. Their Act II turning point came way too late," or, "This would be good if there was actual character development." The bad writing causes me to pick apart and analyze the storytelling, trying to figure out a better way the story could be told.

Ideas generally come in two flavors: premise and character. Premise is your big picture, the overall concept of your story. Here are

some examples of movie premises:
- "The Wizard of Oz" — there is a world in which witches and talking animals are real.
- "Raiders of the Lost Ark" — the Ark of the Covenant exists.
- "Jaws" — there is a man-eating shark.
- "It's a Wonderful Life"— guardian angels protect people.

A premise is the basic idea that your story revolves around. If you don't already have a notebook or file filled with a list of premises, then don't worry. There are lots of ways you can come up with one. For starters, you can do what I do: expose yourself to a whole bunch of storytelling and see if anything jumps out at you. Of course, if you have a life, then finding the time to do all that I do means you'll probably sleep about as much as I do, which isn't much at all.

The next obvious answer is to look at yourself and your own life. What inspires you? What are you passionate about? A good friend who is a fitness instructor wanted me to help her write a short story, only she didn't have an idea yet. She just knew she wanted it to be a period piece. So in her case, she actually had a setting, and we used it to figure out the premise of her story. After working with her, she ended up writing a Victorian thriller about an obese, demon-summoning priest who dies from a stroke. No, it didn't win any awards. But hey, she finished it, and at the end of the journey, she was a better writer for it.

If coming up with a basic premise first isn't working for you, then try focusing on a character. Examples of characters from the movie examples above are:

- "The Wizard of Oz" — a teenage girl with authority issues
- "Raiders of the Lost Ark" — a college professor who moonlights as an archeologist
- "Jaws" — a man who is terrified of the ocean
- "It's a Wonderful Life" — a family man who's sick of his life

When trying to come up with character ideas, don't overthink it. Don't worry about archetypes and fancy writing theories. Just think about either a good guy or a bad guy who interests you. I don't recommend basing a character completely on someone you know, but there's nothing wrong with letting the people you interact with inspire your characters.

There also are times when neither character nor premise is the first thing that sparks your imagination. I have a comic book writer friend who swears that the only way he comes up with ideas is by keeping a travel journal. He travels the country doing book signings, and in every town or city he visits, he sees the major sites and keeps a journal of them. I have another friend who gets his ideas only from listening to music. That doesn't work for me because I'm tone deaf, but for him it works perfectly.

If you are into politics or are a big news junky, then maybe listening to pundits or reading The Washington Post will inspire you. The point is that you need to first pick something that interests you. Don't pick an idea because you think it will sell or because its specific genre is hot right now. Popular tastes change on a dime, and what's hot now may not be three years from. What I'm getting at is that there is no right or wrong way to come up with ideas, but if you want to make it easier on yourself, expose yourself to different stories, people and places, and choose something you are passionate about.

"Virgin Dad"

There are generally three elements that come into play when a person sits in a classroom. There is the individual student, the teacher and the other students. By reading this book you are the student, and by writing this book I am the teacher. The only problem with this setup is that being in a classroom with other students really helps with the writing process. To combat that problem, this book will be structured in a slightly odd way. I'll be writing a fake screenplay so that you can see real examples as I come across them. Sometimes things will work perfectly, and sometimes I'll stumble. But that's OK. The writing process isn't smooth, and I want you to see that even an experienced writer doesn't write a perfect first draft.

"Virgin Dad" is a gag from one of the first screenplays I ever wrote. The screenplay is very meta, and there is a scene in which a character names several fake movie titles. One of those titles is "Virgin Dad." It was a throwaway joke. I liked it because it sounded like a horrible name for a movie but at the same time like it could be an actual studio film. It was never meant to be a story that I would actually write, because the name alone is so ridiculously bad. Little did I know that one day, in writing this book, that's exactly what I would be doing.

For the sake of this book, I thought writing "Virgin Dad" with you guys watching would be awesome, because it's not an intellectual property I'm already invested in. That means I'm not worried about showing off for you guys. I can go through the stages of writing it and be honest without feeling self-conscious. Plus, at this point, it's nothing more than a raw idea. Sure, I could use one of my previously written screenplays or one of my published books, but the problem is that those stories are done. They are birthed and out in the world. They also have been written and rewritten more times than I can count, whereas "Virgin Dad" at this state is nothing more than a movie title. I don't even have a basic premise or character. That makes it the perfect story to write along with you guys, because I'm in the exact same stage you are — I'm starting with nothing.

OK, that's not completely true. I'm not starting with *absolutely* nothing. I have a title, and that title says a lot. "Virgin Dad" — it makes you think, because how could a man be a father but also still a virgin? Off the top of my head, there are two easy answers. The first is that the man donated sperm at some point in his life. He was probably an awkward guy and thus never had a real relationship with someone. The other option is that the man donated sperm and then went into the clergy, so he never had the opportunity to have a relationship. Either way works, and we'll figure that out later. The point is that we now have an idea. "Virgin Dad" is the story of a male virgin who ironically has a child.

Assignment Time

Come up with a working title for your script.

You thought I was going to tell you that you had to come up with an idea for a movie? Nope. That's too easy. I want you to come up with a name for your movie. The road you take to get to the working title of your script is up to you. You can come up with a premise and use that to come up with a title. Or you can come up with a character and use them to inspire a title.

Just keep in mind that the title is a working title. It's what you are going to call your screenplay, and no one else on the planet has to hear the name. Then, once you've written your first draft and do a few rewrites, you can change it all you want. But for now, just come up with a title, and make sure it is inspired by your ideas. If the name is something like "Walking Through Water" but the story is about a quirky waitress working at a truck stop, then that's bad. Remember, the title needs to be *derived from* your ideas. So if your story is about a quirky waitress working at a poolside bar, then "Walking Through Water" would be an OK title.

CHAPTER TWO

Writing the Elevator Pitch

Ever since I was a wee lad, I've hated the phrase "You are what you eat." My problem is that I thought it was true. When I was 6, I spent an entire week refusing to eat anything but food from Dragon Tail, the local Chinese restaurant. My plan was to eat enough dragon tails that I'd grow wings and become a half-dragon/half-boy. My plan never panned out, and I learned then and there that sayings aren't always true.

On the flip side, a saying I wholeheartedly believe in is "You are what you write." When you write, you are taking a little bit of yourself and putting it to paper or, in most of our cases, into very specific sets of ones and zeroes that are squashed into a file.

Writing is personal. If you aren't a newbie, then you already know what I mean. If you are new to writing, then make sure you embrace this. When you spend hundreds of hours with characters inside a world you created, you bond with them. You begin to care about them. The world and the things that live in it become your babies.

This is often a real problem in a classroom environment, because any comment or criticism in front of an audience feels like a stab to the heart. But we'll talk a little more about the attachments formed in writing down the road. For now, just make sure you meld as much as you can with your story, because you're birthing it and it reflects who you are.

The Elevator Pitch

I remember the first time I pitched. I was in Little League, and our main pitcher tore his Adam's apple. As a result, our coach put me into the game...

OK, OK, OK — I never played Little League. I was in Brownies, but that's a whole other story. The type of pitching I want to talk about involves trying to sell your story to someone else.

Specifically, we are going to be focusing on the elevator pitch, which is sometimes called a log line. I know it sounds odd to be worrying about pitching your idea when you've not written a single thing, but we are using the concept of a pitch as a tool for writing your script, not selling your screenplay.

So what is an elevator pitch? It's a synopsis that's short enough for you to say to someone on an elevator ride between two floors. It should introduce the key elements of your story, it should be interesting enough to hook the listener so they will want more, and it should clearly establish the tone and genre of your screenplay.

Here are several pitches for some well-known movies. Take note of what information is included and how it is presented.

- After a twister transports a lonely Kansas farm girl to a magical land, she sets out on a dangerous journey to find a wizard with

the power to send her home. Standing in her way is a wicked witch who more than anything else in the world wants her shoes.
- A world-famous archeologist spends half his time wearing a tweed jacket and teaching at a university and the other half going on incredible deadly adventures to retrieve lost treasures. Contacted by the CIA, he has to stop the Nazis from discovering the Ark of the Covenant and using it to take over the world.
- After a series of grisly shark attacks, a sheriff struggles to protect his small beach community from the bloodthirsty monster in spite of the town's greedy chamber of commerce.
- A family man struggles to escape his small American town for a more successful life in the big city. When his constant efforts fail, he contemplates suicide. But his guardian angel visits, and the man experiences what the world would be like if he had never been born.
- The world is invaded by extradimensional aliens, and it's up to a supersoldier displaced from time to lead a team of superpowered loners into battle to defeat them.

Answer Key: "The Wizard of Oz," "Raiders of the Lost Ark," "Jaws," "It's a Wonderful Life," "The Avengers"

All of the pitches above clearly have several things in common: They introduce the basic premise. They tell us who the story is about (the protagonist). They tell us what the protagonist wants (the goal). And they explain what stands in the protagonist's way (the antagonist).

Coming into this chapter you should already have an idea for a story, which means you should already know one of the key elements of your pitch. As I break down each of these points, make sure you are thinking about your story in the back of your head — because if you've not already guessed, your assignment for this chapter will be to write your own pitch.

The Protagonist

The protagonist is your main character, whose point of view you normally expect the audience to share. He or she is the person your story is about. If you were doing a formal log line in Hollywood, you probably wouldn't use your character's name when writing a pitch (like in the examples above), because unless a character is based on someone famous, their name is irrelevant. Instead, you should use broadly identifying traits and flaws, such as "dirty politician," "liberal judge," "angst-ridden teenager" or "hopeless romantic." However, for our exercise, it helps to use your main character's name. Once you've named them, you will start to identify with them.

After you've named your character, I still want you to give them some sort of defining trait. Be very careful when choosing your adjectives. You don't just want words that pop; you want an accurate description that really represents your main character. Eventually the trait will represent your protagonist's main flaw, but we'll get to that in a later chapter.

The Goal

The next thing your character needs is a goal. In real life, every person has a want or a need, and in writing, you should make sure your characters also have one as well. To make things even more complicated, your character also should have a specific goal in individual scenes and even pieces of dialogue. But for our pitch, we don't need to worry about those kinds of desires or goals. For the moment, we are only going to look at the big picture.

We want to figure out the protagonist's main driving force. What is the one thing they want more than anything else? Looking at the examples above, Dorothy wants to go home, Indiana Jones wants to find the Ark of the Covenant, Martin Brody wants to stop the shark killings, George Bailey wants to be a successful businessman and Captain America wants to stop an alien invasion.

So really think about the one thing your character wants, and that's what your script will be about. Your protagonist will be trying to achieve this goal, but something will interfere. What's getting in their way (other than their own major flaw)? The antagonist!

The Antagonist

Let's be clear for a moment. When I say "antagonist," I don't simply mean "the bad guy." Sure, the antagonist could be a villain, but an antagonist also can be any force that stops the protagonist from getting what they want. In disaster movies ("Armageddon," "The Perfect Storm," "Dante's Peak," etc.) the antagonist is a force of nature rather than a human character. In romantic comedies there are two protagonists who do double duty, serving as antagonists to each other.

So the first thing you need to decide is what exactly is preventing your protagonist from getting what they want. Is it another character? Is it wealth or social status? Is it the environment? This sets up the central conflict, which will drive your story and your pitch.

The Pitch

As I explained in the last chapter, I'll be writing a screenplay alongside of you so that you can watch me go through the writing process, follow the kinds of missteps I take and see how I later correct them. So what I know right now about my story is this:

- Title: "Virgin Dad"
- Premise: a movie about a guy who is a virgin but ends up having a kid.

That's all I know. So the next thing I'm supposed to figure out is who the story is about. I know the guy is in his early to mid-30s and he is socially awkward, but that's it. So let's give him a name. I'm going with Simon. I may change that later, but for now it's a good starting place. In this context, Simon has an almost nerdy feel, probably because I think of the chipmunk or the character from "The Mortal Instruments."

So what does Simon want in life? The obvious answer is that he wants to get laid. However, I don't think that's the kind of movie I want to write. It's been done before: "American Pie," The 40-Year-Old Virgin" and a bunch of other movies. That's not saying that those are bad movies or that you shouldn't write something similar. It's that at this point I know my voice, and that type of story simply isn't my thing.

I grew up watching "Dawson's Creek," "Buffy the Vampire Slayer" and "Felicity," and as a result I seem to enjoy more angsty teen stuff. That means for this screenplay, I probably want a story that is more quirky and cute as opposed to raunchy. "Stranger than Fiction" and "Little Miss Sunshine" pop into my mind in terms of the tone and feel I'm after. Since that is the kind of story I want to tell, Simon's goal needs to fit into that genre.

We know that Simon is socially awkward. That's his defining character trait right now, though it may change later. In my head, what I see for his personality is more of an arrogant nerd than an awkward dork. For example, I see him working at a research facility or somewhere he can focus only on his thing with little human interaction. I don't see him as the kind of guy who gets nervous talking to the barista at Starbucks. He wouldn't waste his time going to Starbucks. He's the kind of guy who owns a French press and brews his own coffee to the precise temperature required for the perfect cup.

So if that's what I see in him, what would he want in life? Right now I'm guessing that whatever he's doing at work, he's about to hit a big breakthrough or score a huge government grant — something that would be epic in his field. I'll figure that out in a bit.

So now we know the following:
- Title: "Virgin Dad"
- Protagonist: Simon, who is socially awkward
- Protagonist's goal: a big breakthrough at work

So the next thing we need is an antagonist, something to get in the way of Simon getting what he wants. For starters, Simon will get in his own way. That's part of the fun with flaws: you'll discover that no matter what your protagonist wants, they will always be their own mini-antagonist.

But your protagonist still needs a *real* antagonist besides himself. The only exception would be a movie like "Fight Club," where there are issues of self-perception and split personality. In my case, I have an obvious antagonist built into my premise. The movie is about Simon learning he's a father. That means his kid is going to enter his life and screw everything up. His kid is going to be the antagonist!

Don't forget that "antagonist" doesn't mean "bad guy." It's not necessarily the villain, unless you are writing more of an action-adventure piece. The antagonist is just the force stopping the hero from getting what he wants. So the kid doesn't have to be a bad kid. It just has to be someone who conflicts with Simon.

I know right away that I want the kid to be a girl. I like creating female characters. I particularly like writing strong female characters. Since Simon is socially awkward, I know I want the daughter to be a fearless spitfire, setting up a classic "Odd Couple" syndrome. Their personalities right off the bat will cause major conflict. As for a name, let's call her Meta. I know it sounds weird, but I want her name to be a modern version of a hippie name, like Tweet or Like. So I'll call her Meta for now, but I might rename her when we get to character creation.

What we have now is:
- Title: "Virgin Dad"
- Protagonist: Simon, who is socially awkward
- Protagonist's goal: a big breakthrough at work
- Antagonist: Meta, Simon's spunky daughter

If I combined those elements, it would look something like this:

Simon Baker, a socially awkward 35-year-old researcher, makes the discovery of a lifetime. But before he can prove it, his world is turned upside down when Meta, his sperm-donation daughter, arrives.

All the elements are there. It's a complete sentence. Looks good, right? Well…

It has the pieces, but it doesn't really get across what I want it to get across. A pitch also must express the genre and tone of the piece. If it's a love story, that should be clear in the pitch. If it's a noir crime story, then the pitch should say so. If it's an action-adventure piece, that should be obvious. In my case, I want this to say "quirky comedy."

So how do you make the genre and tone clear? Think about your audience. Who will watch your movie? Are your viewers going to be more literary types who enjoy art-house films? Will your screenplay have tons of explosions? Maybe the people who will want to watch your movie enjoy slow-paced, slice-of-life films?

I know it seems blasphemous to think about marketing before you've even written something, but doing so helps define what tone your movie will have. I'm going for a quirky comedy, so other movies that come to mind are "Juno" or "Little Miss Sunshine," and if that's the tone I want to come across in my pitch, I need to add a little bit of quirkiness and fun to it. So with that in mind, I could rework what I had before like this:

> Simon Baker, a 35-year-old virgin and robotics expert, is about to settle a $20 million contract with the Department of Defense when he discovers he has a 12-year-old test-tube daughter.

So what's changed in this draft? Well, for one, I gave Simon a specific job. Why? I decided he's not a virgin because he *can't* get laid — he's a virgin because, although he wants human connection, he doesn't have time to mess with that junk. His work is more important to him. Since I know human interaction is going to be a problem for him, making him an expert in artificial intelligence seems like a nice contrast.

Looking at this rewrite, we can see that I now have a much better description of who Simon is — all of which I made up on the fly when writing the pitch. In addition to defining who he is, I also added the "12-year-old test-tube daughter" bit. It's enough of a hook to grab attention, and it adds a fun, almost ironic tone to the pitch. So now it's clear what type of story I'm trying to tell.

That being said, it's still a little sloppy. I really want to punch it up and make it grab attention. I want my potential audience to read the pitch and want to know more. I'm also not happy with the overall sentence structure and wording. So let's take another stab at it:

> Up for a $20 million robotics contract with the Department of Defense, 35-year-old virgin Simon Baker has to juggle his career with the discovery that he has a 12-year-old test-tube daughter named Meta.

I could still rewrite it again, and if I were using the pitch to actually sell the story to someone, I definitely would rewrite it. But as a writing example, it does what I need it to do: it gives me all the major plot elements and sets up the story.

Assignment Time

Write a pitch for your screenplay. Make sure you include the four major points: premise, protagonist, protagonist's goal and antagonist. Also make sure the tone of your story is clear.

The best part about using an elevator pitch as a writing tool is that it's really easy to check whether you've messed up anywhere. Let's look at my finished pitch for "Virgin Dad."

> Up for a $20 million robotics contract with the Department of Defense, 35-year-old virgin Simon Baker has to juggle his career with the discovery that he has a 12-year-old test-tube daughter named Meta.

Who is the pitch about?

> Up for a $20 million robotics contract with the Department of Defense, **35-year-old virgin Simon Baker** has to juggle his career with the discovery that he has a 12-year-old test-tube daughter named Meta.

What does the protagonist want?

Up for a $20 million robotics contract with the Department of Defense, 35-year-old virgin Simon Baker has to juggle his career with the discovery that he has a 12-year-old test-tube daughter named Meta.

What's getting in his way?

Up for a $20 million robotics contract with the Department of Defense, 35-year-old virgin Simon Baker has to juggle his career with the discovery that he has a 12-year-old test-tube daughter named **Meta**.

What is the tone of the story?

Up for a $20 million robotics contract with the Department of Defense, 35-year-old virgin Simon Baker has to juggle his career with the discovery that **he has a 12-year-old test-tube daughter** named Meta.

By going in reverse, I can double check that my elevator pitch has all the things it is supposed to have.

CHAPTER THREE

CHARACTER CREATION

I live in a geek world, especially because of how involved I am in the comic book industry, but for some reason I'm not a true geek. How do I know? I've never played "Dungeons and Dragons."

Recently I attended my first gaming convention. I went with several board game designers, and the car ride took more than 10 hours. One thing that came up was how I had never played D&D. I told them that although I enjoy creating fictional characters, I like to be myself. It's why theater and acting never intrigued me. I enjoy being onstage in front of people, but when I am, I want to be me. I don't want to be a character.

The discussion quickly derailed into which one of my friends would be the Dungeon Master and prep a game in which the premise involved me being sucked into the D&D fantasy world. This led to my admission that I am not a fan of being dirty, which they found very amusing. I'm not a neat freak or OCD, but I'm as close as you can get without crossing that line. So they were thinking up all these weird scenarios in which I would be sneezed on by a giant or pooped on by a dragon. Then they would giggle like little girls at the cringing sounds I made as their ideas got grosser and grosser.

The point is that by the end of the whole thing, they had more or less created a Scott King character who, although similar to me, wasn't really who I am. From a writing standpoint, they had created a fairly well-fleshed-out character. They gave the fictional me a goal: wanting to get back to the present where indoor plumbing exists. They gave me a flaw: having way too big of an ego that borders on pure hubris. They also gave me a lot of little quirks, such as a really dry, sarcastic sense of humor and the desire to not get dirty.

When you're creating your characters, I don't suggest basing them on yourself. That usually ends badly. But don't hesitate to look at the people around you for inspiration.

What Makes Up a Character?

There is no magic formula or secret trick for how to create a compelling and interesting character. At our core, people are the same. We all have wants and we all have needs. At the most basic level, we want to live, we want to eat, we want to survive. What separates me from you are our personalities and experiences.

Experiences are pretty easy to comprehend. They're the events of a person's life that make them who they are. Was your character born to a well-off family? Did they go to a private preschool? Were their parents drug addicts? Did they get picked on in elementary school? Were they popular in high school? Did they have friends? Did a friend ever severely hurt them? How bad was their first breakup?

It's your job as a writer to create your character, and one of the ways to get started is to figure out all the key events of your character's life, from the time they were born until the start of your story. Many writers start their character creation by writing a biography.

But it's not just the facts that matter. You also need to get inside of your character's head. For example, let's go back to the issue of bullying. Let's say your character was really crapped on in elementary school. How did they deal with it? Did they run and hide? Did they spend years of their life in fear of being bullied? Did they get angry? Did they fight back?

As you start to figure out the key events of your character's life, you'll also start to flesh out their personality. And in the end, it's their personality that leads them to the choices they make.

Don't get me wrong — the facts are nice to know. I'm sure there will be a situation in which it's interesting to know a character's favorite color is maroon, but it really isn't helpful. However, what if maroon is the color of their father's motorcycle, which the character watched their father rebuild from scratch, and thus they associate that color with the love they have for their parent? Yes, that was a cheeseball example, but you get the idea.

What's In a Name?

If you want to get formal, there are a whole slew of rules when it comes to naming characters. Here are few:
- Don't give characters names that start with the same letter, like Tim and Tony.
- Don't give characters similar-sounding names, like Sammy and Tammy.
- Don't use alliteration, like Mary-Margret.
- Use root words to give the names of your characters more meaning.

However, here's the thing with names. You're better off saying "screw you" to the rules and simply picking names that mean something to you — names that speak to you.

As of right now, the protagonist of "Virgin Dad" is Simon Baker. I'm not OK with that. Simon was simply a placeholder name, and now it's time to really name him. Naming a character can be a tough thing for many people. I don't normally get stuck on it, but I am now, and that's probably because "Virgin Dad" isn't my dream writing gig. It's not something that's been sitting in the back of my head for months or years like most of my writing projects.

Naming your character can be as simple or as complicated as you make it. Theoretically, I could stick with Simon, but I don't want to. It doesn't feel right. So what does feel right? I know I like the name Dexter. It's nerdy and fun, but the TV show is so well known and well done that the name no longer feels original. I love the name Milton, but I already have a nerdy character named that in another project, so I don't want to use that here. So what do I do?

Honestly, I Google baby names. In this case, I just typed in "most popular boy baby names." This is what showed up:

- Jacob
- Mason
- William
- Jayden
- Noah
- Michael
- Ethan
- Alexander
- Aiden
- Daniel

- Anthony
- Matthew
- Elijah
- Joshua
- Liam
- Andrew
- James
- David
- Benjamin
- Logan

    I don't like any of them. Jacob makes me think of "Twilight." Mason sounds like the name of a detective in a crime thriller. William is too serious and hoity-toity. Jayden is too cool. Noah is too biblical for my story. Michael is too generic. And I could keep going.

    So I can either keep Googling names or I can do something else. In my case, I know Simon is supposed to be smart and have something to do with research. So I'm going to cheat. When I think science and research, I think of CERN, the big research company famous for its particle accelerator. A quick Google search led me to its staff page, and here are some of the names there:

- François de Rose
- Francis Farley
- Heribert Koziol
- Rafel Carreras
- Paolo Zanella
- Eugene Carlos
- Nicolas Koulberg
- Violette Brisson
- Jack Steinberger

- Herwig Schopper
- Carlo Rubbia
- Jürgen Schukraft
- Robert Cailliau
- Ugo Amaldi
- Marzio Nessi
- Francesca Nessi-Tedaldi
- Robert Eisenstein
- Hafeez Hoorani
- Alvaro De Rújula

Look at those names! Those are great names. Way better than just a list of baby names. In this case, my eyes immediately went to Eugene. Eugene Baker. It sounds OK but still isn't quite right. We have to remember that Eugene, formerly Simon, is a big nerd who spent tons of time in school, so his full name should be Dr. Eugene Baker, ScD. To me, the "ScD" is important. It stands for "doctor of science," and in academia it is ranked higher than a PhD.

Dr. Eugene Baker, ScD

Now that I know Eugene's name, the next thing I want to do is figure out what he looks like. I already know he's 35. I also see him as slightly above-average height. I'm picturing him at 6-foot-1. This is important because he's the kind of guy who's always looking down at others. He thinks he is smarter than everyone else, and I want that to be reflected visually so that at times he is towering over the other characters.

For race, I'm picturing Eugene as a white guy, but if this movie were ever to be actually made, it wouldn't matter who they cast in the part. For the character we are creating, he could easily be of any race or nationality. On the flip side, when we move on to his daughter Meta, I'm pretty sure I want her to be something other than Caucasian.

For build, I want Eugene to be the kind of guy that can eat anything and never gain a pound. He's that guy you hate because he's super skinny and has a mutant metabolism.

For hair, I want Eugene to have a head that looks like a big curly mop. It will be light brown and unkempt most of the time. Although he's particular about his stuff, he considers grooming a logical waste of time, because as soon as he goes to bed or is exposed to humidity, his hair will go crazy anyway.

And I think that's good. I can picture Eugene. I know what he looks like. Sure, I could get super specific and go into his eye color and what his jaw line or stubble look like, but you need to remember that we are writing a screenplay. It means that those kind of decisions will be made by a director and the casting department. So instead of picking purely physical descriptions for your character, make sure all your character's traits add to their personality.

Create Personality

Personality is a big one. It's *who your character is*. When creating personality, you should always choose a starting point. In the case of Eugene, I already decided he's an uber nerd, so I was able to build upon that and create a name and look that matches his personality.

One of my favorite things to do with students is have someone pull out their cell phone and scroll through their contact list. Then I wait for the person to make a face. Sometimes it's a smile. Sometimes it's an eye roll. Other times it's a wince. Once I get a reaction, I ask the student why they made the face.

In one case, a female student got really angry. She furrowed her brows and made a grunting noise. When I asked her to explain, she said the name that made her react so strongly was her sister's fiance. Apparently the guy was a no-good nothing. He had no job, no aspirations — he was a slug who contributed nothing to society. So I asked her to describe the guy using only one word, and she said "dirty." Working from that, similar to the way we used "uber nerdy" for Eugene, she was able to create a character who became the antagonist in her romantic comedy.

So if you are struggling with your character's personality, pick one defining trait (which you were supposed to do in the last chapter!) and build upon it until you have a better idea of who your character is.

Get to Know Your Protagonist

Spoiler alert: Your assignment for this chapter will be to write a character biography for your protagonist and your antagonist, but first I want you guys to watch as I do them both for Eugene.

When creating a character biography, it's important to write in first person. For example, I wouldn't write, "Eugene was born in 1492," because that's third person. Instead I would write, "I was born in 1492," because I would be pretending to be Eugene.

The other important thing to keep in mind about this assignment is not spending too much time overthinking it. We want gut reactions so that we can start to get to know our characters. After we do a first draft, then we can go back and clean it up and tweak things. But for the first go-around, make sure your character biography is done in a free-form style.

I honestly *hate* writing in first person, so I'm going to cheat on this assignment. Instead of doing a diary entry or something for

Eugene, I'm going to interview him. I'm going to pretend that I'm a local reporter doing a story about him. I'm also going to pretend that I didn't do proper research, so I really don't know much about who he is.

If I also didn't want to do a Q&A, I could write a dating profile or something similar. They key remains writing in first person. And make sure you talk about the character's background and history.

Q&A Part 1:
- Scott: Hey, Eugene, it's —
- Eugene: Doctor.
- Scott: Excuse me?
- Eugene: It's Dr. Eugene Baker.
- Scott: Oh, sorry. What kind of doctor? Like head-shrink doctor or turn-your-head-and-cough doctor?
- Eugene: I did not spend 12 years in postdoctoral programs so that I could be compared to a mere medical practitioner or psychologist. Neither field is real science anyway.
- Scott: Ohhh, OK then. So moving forward, I'm here to talk to you about your grant or something?
- Eugene: Grant? No, not a grant. Grants are miniscule. What I'm about to bring in is 20 million dollars. That's —

OK, I just stopped writing. Everything above took me about a minute. Why did I stop? Because I want Eugene to respond with something like, "That's a stack of single dollar bills that would reach all the way to the moon." I don't know if that's true or not, so I'm going to do some quick research and math.

A dollar bill is .011 cm thick. A mile is 5,280 feet, which equals 160,934.4 centimeters. So a one-mile stack of dollar bills would be about $14,630,400. Since the moon is roughly 240,000 miles away, it would take a lot more than 20 million bucks to reach it. So let me go back and tweak Eugene's response.

Q&A Part 2:
- Eugene: What I'm about to bring in is 20 million dollars. If you stacked that in dollar bills, it would be more than a mile tall, which is probably more than what you walk in a day.
- Scott: Hey, are you calling me fat?
- Eugene: I'm merely making a hypothesis about your rotund nature. Theoretically, you may walk more than a mile a day, but if that's the case then your caloric intake is —
- Scott: That's it. I'm done. I'm not writing an article about you. I'm out of here.
- Eugene: Now wait just a minute. I meant no offense. I'm sorry if my candor was taken wrong, and I think you would be making a mistake if you left.
- Scott: Yeah? And why's that?
- Eugene: Because if my contract comes in for 20 million dollars, this whole department will be saved. It's huge news, and the whole campus needs to know about it.
- Scott: Fine, but I want something good.
- Eugene: Like what?
- Scott: Something real. Something personal. Something that will make our readers care about you and see you as human.
- Eugene: I like to butter my toast bottom-side down.
- Scott: No, no, no, no. That's not what I mean. I want to really get to know you, like where you are from and how you became you. OK?
- Eugene: I don't like to talk about my upbringing, but since one

day this interview may be an important historical document, I can see the merits in it. OK, ask away.

I just stopped writing again. Why? Well, Eugene and I got off on the wrong foot. He was a hostile and kind of mean character. As a result, the scene was a ton of fun to write, but it wasn't really helpful in getting to know Eugene. So I shifted the direction of the scene so that Eugene would be less hostile to my questions.

Q&A Part 3:

- Scott: Where were you born?
- Eugene: I was born here in Washington, D.C. And should I ever be elected president, I will be the first ever born in our nation's capital.
- Scott: Is that something you'd want — to be president?
- Eugene: No, not particularly, though I think I would make a great president.
- Scott: So what do you want?
- Eugene: I want to get the contract from the Department of Defense and save our program. I also want to use the money to further my research in artificial intelligence and win the Nobel Prize.
- Scott: So science and furthering knowledge are important to you?
- Eugene: Yes.
- Scott: When did that start?
- Eugene: What do you mean?
- Scott: When was the first time you can remember being into science and learning?
- Eugene: When I was 6, my father gave me the Perceptor Transformer toy for Christmas. It was an Autobot — I wouldn't

have played with it if it had been a Decepticon — and it transformed into a low-powered working microscope.
- Scott: That's really cool.
- Eugene: Yes, well it did tide me over until I could save up enough money from my chores to buy a real microscope.
- Scott: What do your parents think of your accomplishments now?
- Eugene: They think nothing. They are dead.
- Scott: I'm sorry.
- Eugene: They died a long time ago. Don't be sorry. I don't know why people always say "sorry" when you tell them a parent has passed away.
- Scott: So if your parents died when you were young, who raised you?
- Eugene: I raised myself.
- Scott: You lived on the streets and had no home, or what?
- Eugene: No, I lived with my cousin —

This is interesting. I hadn't planned this. In the back of my mind, I knew something happened to Eugene when he was young. For some reason I knew human connections weren't important to him. But until this interview, I didn't know why. Now I do. His parents died when he was a child, which truly scarred him and made it so that he didn't develop proper relationships with people.

Even cooler is that Eugene just gave me a supporting character that I didn't know existed. Eugene has a cousin! That's great. I'll have her be a girl and the complete opposite of Eugene. So she will be warm and sweet and fun and outgoing.

Q&A Part 4:
- Scott: You lived on the streets and had no home, or what?

- Eugene: No, I lived with my cousin and her parents.
- Scott: So your aunt and uncle?
- Eugene: Technically that is how you would label our biological relationship, but we were never what you would call "close."
- Scott: What about your cousin? What's your relationship with her?
- Eugene: Chloey is the most obnoxious and illogical person I've ever met.
- Scott: So you don't keep in touch?
- Eugene: Oh, no, she lives a block away from my apartment. In fact, I can't seem to get rid of her. She's always doing what she can to help out, which often leads to her getting in the way.
- Scott: Well, it sounds like she cares about you.
- Eugene: She does. It's just she does not understand how important my time is and how hard it is to make time for weekly movie nights or trips to parasitic-bacteria-infected places like the bowling alley.

All right, I think that's it. I wrote two full pages of this interview, but there's no reason for me to make you read the rest of it. I think you get the idea about the point of this assignment. It's to make this stuff up on the fly and use it to get to know your character better.

Assignment Time

Write a two-page biography for your protagonist and your antagonist.

Make sure you write the biography in first person, and make sure it's more than just a list of facts. It should be done in such a way that reveals character. Remember, if you don't want to write a straightforward diary or journal, maybe try doing a Q&A like I did, or create a dating profile.

Did you do your biography? When you go back and read it, is it a list of boring stuff like your character's favorite color? Or is it revealing, like how we learned Eugene's parents died or that he's still close with his cousin? If your biographies are just a list, then go back and redo them. If they do reveal character, then you're golden and can move forward!

CHAPTER FOUR

CHARACTER ARCS

I'm not an only child. I have a sister who is six years younger than I am, and she drives me crazy. There is one memory of her I have growing up that really defines who she is. It's great and my most vivid memory of her as a child. It's so strong that I'm going to steal it for Meta.

Granddaddy, my grandfather on my mother's side of the family, would watch us off and on because after my parents divorced, we lived with him and my mother for a time. He was never good with kids, and he was one of the most stubborn people I've ever met in my life. That stubbornness was passed down to my sister.

My sister was cute at 5 years old. She had curly blond hair and the biggest smile ever. She also was addicted to sweets. On this particular day, for whatever reason, she got it into her head that she wanted chocolate. So after lunch she asked Granddaddy if she could have some chocolate. He said no because we didn't have any and instead offered her an orange Popsicle.

She took the Popsicle, which was in a bowl because Granddaddy was horribly terrified we'd mess up his carpets or marble floors with stains. Now as adorable as my sister was, she wasn't the smartest kid, so it's no surprise that her plan to get chocolate would have no logical steps.

She took the pepper shaker off the table and started sprinkling pepper on her Popsicle. Granddaddy saw her and asked, "What the f* are you doing?"

Kaitlyn, very daintily and ladylike, smiled and said, "Oh, Granddaddy, you shouldn't use that language. Mommy doesn't like it. And as for what I'm doing, this is how I like to eat my Popsicles."

Granddaddy looked at me and asked, "Is she serious?"

I told him, "I don't know. It's Kaitlyn. But if I were you, I wouldn't let her eat it." So Granddaddy smirked and told her that she wasn't allowed to waste the Popsicle. Kaitlyn said she wasn't going to and proceeded to eat the whole thing.

Now, I've never seen anyone hit with pepper spray, but I'm sure it's something close to what my sister experienced. She devoured the peppered Popsicle and almost immediately started coughing and crying. Thick mucus was pouring from her eyes and from her nose. It was *disgusting*.

Granddaddy didn't know what to do, but his best idea was to get her water to rinse off her face with. In hindsight, if she had been sprayed with pepper or something, that would've made sense. But she had eaten a significant amount of pepper, which is totally different. So I have no idea why, but he picked her up, carried her outside and threw her into the pool. Of course she was coughing and crying so much that she couldn't swim, and then he had to go in after her.

They stayed in the pool for a good 30 minutes, and when Kaitlyn had finally finished crying, she looked at Granddaddy and said, "I'd really like some chocolate now." He felt so guilty that we went to the store and bought her a hundred dollars worth of chocolate, making her promise to never tell my mother what had happened.

What's important to note about that whole incident is that, as a character, my 5-year-old sister was pretty spot on. She had a want: chocolate. Granddaddy didn't want to get her chocolate. This caused conflict, about which Kaitlyn wasn't passive. She formed a plan to get her chocolate. The plan worked too well and she paid a price, but ultimately she got what she wanted.

Character Arcs

I don't like ultimatums or all-inclusive statements, but if I had to boil down movies, or storytelling in general, I'd say there is one single most important thing: character.

Stories are not just things that happen. They are about a person going through a series of events and about how those events either change or don't change that person. This change is refereed to as a "character arc," and every protagonist needs one. Why? Well, in real life people change as they grow. Very rarely can you say that you are the exact same person you were 10 years ago. On the same note, it's harder for people to change as they grow older. The big exception to this is trauma. Living through a traumatic event can drastically change a person.

So think of your story as a traumatic event. It's something so big and so grand that, when all is said and done, your character won't be the same person as when they started. The events of your story must somehow change them.

As a writer, your job is to develop a character. If you do it right, then the changes in your character will seem to happen naturally as your story progresses. If you do it wrong, then the arc will feel forced and you'll be accused of having bad character development. (We'll talk more about this when we get to structure).

The most common way to show a character arc is to illustrate the character's most pronounced flaw and have them fix it by the end of the story. A perfect example is the movie "Liar Liar." It's a traditional studio comedy, and in it Jim Carrey's character goes through a very traditional arc. When the movie starts off, we see that he is a massive liar. He lies in court. He lies to his children. He lies to his ex-wife. He's a liar — lying is his flaw. So what happens? Well, by the end of the movie he discovers that lying so much is wrong, and he turns over a new leaf by becoming an honest person.

It's not award-winning writing, but for the average moviegoer it works. Why does it work, even being as simple as it is? Because audiences today have been trained for decades to understand that this is how storytelling works. Most movies, books and comics use character arcs in this way.

You want another example? Think of Tom Cruise's character in "Rain Man." A greedy car dealer, he kidnaps his autistic brother because he feels cheated for not receiving any money in his father's will, while his brother received a fortune. By the end of the movie, he's grown to love his brother and realizes the importance of family. This is proven when he has the choice to take the money but instead turns it down.

There are, of course, exceptions to character arcs. For example, in a long franchise it's not uncommon to have the main protagonist stay the same while the supporting characters drastically change or grow. Or maybe your protagonist is an anti-hero. They go through the whole arc but, when all is said and done, they fail in their endeavors, and instead of learning and becoming a better person, they choose to stay they same. You also can have a reverse arc in which the story is about the corruption and fall of a person. There are lots of ways you can use arcs, so don't feel trapped into sticking with a traditional one.

Character Flaws

For your protagonist to undergo a character arc, they have to have a flaw. It may feel odd to create a flawed character, but you need to keep in mind that no one is perfect. Everyone has flaws, which is why your characters need to have flaws — and not just one flaw, but multiple flaws, because that's how people work. We all have flaws, including you!

Personally, I talk a lot, I'm not shy, I'm a neat freak, I have authority issues, I'm sort of weird ... and I could keep going. Think about yourself. What are your flaws? Are you absentminded, blunt, opinionated, impatient or mean? Do you have low self-esteem? Flaws are part of what makes us who we are, and they affect our lives in very drastic ways. Not only do flaws help your character seem more complex, but they also make them relatable. Reading a story about a perfect person is boring.

A great example is the TV show "House." Gregory House is one of the most asshole, dickish characters ever created on TV, but what's crazy is that he is the star of the show! It worked because he was so flawed that it was fascinating to watch.

In addition to giving your character flaws, you also can give them quirks. I'm personally not a big fan of it, but again, we are talking about writing and what works for you. What do I mean by a quirk? Well, maybe your character is a caffeine junkie and they are always drinking coffee. Maybe your character is a shy girl who wears her hair in such a way that it always keeps her face covered? Quirks are real. I have a few and I'm sure you do too. They can be a tool to help make your character more identifiable, but be careful. They can easily be overused or used as a crutch for bad character development.

Are They Likable?

Another thing to keep in mind when creating protagonists is whether they are likable. That's not saying your main character needs to be a good guy. It just means they have to be relatable enough so that your audience will want to keep reading or watching. They have to care about the character.

So how do you make your character more likable? For starters, you create a strong character. You make sure they have realistic flaws. You make sure they feel fleshed out and that their wants and desires are clear.

A very simple way to make your audience care about your protagonist is to hurt them. You see this all the time in romantic comedies. The movie starts off with the main character getting dumped and ending up heartbroken.

Creating likable traits in your character is often referred to as "saving the cat" or "petting the dog." It's that moment in a Superman story when he takes a break from fighting a supervillain to save a cat that's stuck in a tree. Or it's that moment in an election story when the candidate smiles and pets a dog while posing for the cameras. If for some reason you are having trouble making your character likable, you can try giving them a moment like this. Just be careful, because it's very hard to pull off without it seeming cliche.

Wants and Needs

We all have wants and needs, and so should your characters. Normally a protagonist has one main want. In a romantic comedy, they may want to get the girl. In an epic fantasy, they may want to save the world. In a horror movie, they may want to simply survive.

That's good. You should start with one main goal for your character. But like flaws, your character needs more than one big want. Think about yourself. You have long-term goals. Maybe you want to be rich. Maybe you want to be famous. Maybe you want to be a published writer. But you also have short-term wants: Maybe you are hungry so you want to eat. Maybe you're bored at work and you want to leave.

When getting to know your character, you need to keep in mind their immediate wants as well as their long-term goals. Every time your character says something, they need to have a reason for saying it. (I'll expand on this idea more when we talk about dialogue).

Think about your interactions with other people. When you say something, you normally have an intention for saying it. Maybe you are trying to sound smart. Maybe you are trying to make someone laugh. Maybe you are trying to prove yourself right. Maybe you are trying to get someone to like you. Really think about the last conversation you had with someone. Think about the things you said and why you said them.

So you need to make sure you know your character's history, their flaws and the journey, or arc, you want them go on. But you also need to keep in mind the things they want, because it's their wants and needs that motivate them. When people talk about something being "character-driven," they are talking about that motivation. It's when a story moves forward because of the character's needs.

Eugene's Journey

Eugene's flaw is pretty straightforward: he is bad at relationships. He doesn't see the point in them and instead puts his career first. It's why he's never dated and it's why he's still a virgin. The only things that matter to him are his work and the legacy he will leave behind.

This means that over the course of my story, Eugene needs to grow and change. He will become a better person and realize that the only thing that matters in life is your relationships with others.

As for his wants, at the start of the movie he will want to score the big contract with the Department of Defense and then make a name for himself in the world of science. By the end of the movie, his goal will be to be a good father for his daughter.

Pretty simple and straightforward. As for how his transition will happen, we will address that later when we talk about structure, but for now we are at a good place.

Remember Meta?

In "Virgin Dad," Eugene's daughter Meta is our antagonist. The antagonist is just as important as the protagonist, so her goals and wants are just as important as her father's. At the same time, she also should have a flaw as well as an arc. If I was doing an action movie, then maybe giving her an arc wouldn't be important, but because we are doing a quirky drama, her journey and growth matter.

In many ways, character arcs and your character's flaw sum up the theme of your story. So in this case, the theme of "Virgin Dad" would be that family matters. But if it's important for you to write a story about gun control, for example, then the arcs your characters go through would need to reflect that.

In this case, I want Meta's journey to thematically tie into what's going on with her dad. I want her to have trust issues. She doesn't trust anyone — she believes she doesn't need anyone because she can take care of herself. That means that by the end of the movie, she will have learned that yes, it's OK to be independent, but at the same time you can trust people and let them in.

As for Meta's wants, I honestly don't know and haven't spent any time thinking about it yet. I know that she's going to show up in Eugene's life not because she wants to, but because she has to. Then, because she's not a trusting person, her dream world would be one in which she can live and do her own thing without requiring adults for any kind of help. Yeah, yeah, yeah — that's good! Meta wants to be emancipated and to live on her own without any adults! She's only 12, so ultimately she'll be very unhappy with it.

Assignment Time

Come up with the following:
- Know your protagonist's main desire.
- Know your protagonist's main flaw.
- Figure out your protagonist's character arc.
- Know your antagonist's main want.
- Know your antagonist's main flaw.
- If appropriate to the genre of your story, create a character arc for your antagonist.

Did you fully answer the questions above? Not just quick answers, but real ones? Then you're good to go. Here is how I would handle them for "Virgin Dad."

- Eugene's want: He wants to score $20 million in funding and make a huge scientific breakthrough.
- Eugene's flaw: He doesn't believe human relationships are important.
- Eugene's arc: He learns that relationships matter, particularly the importance of being part of a family unit.
- Meta's want: She wants to live on her own without the help of any adults.
- Meta's flaw: She's too independent and doesn't trust anyone.
- Meta's arc: She learns that it's OK to turn to other people, particularly family, for help.

CHAPTER FIVE

Writing The Treatment

Screenwriting is all about storytelling. Because all movies follow a similar structure of setup and payoff, what makes a movie really stand out is the storytelling. How a story is told really matters more than the story itself.

It's why people mocking "high concepts" is silly. A commercial-sounding movie idea may seem like a joke, but if given to a great writer, it could end up being something truly magical.

Look at "The King's Speech." It's the story of a soon-to-be king with a speech impediment hiring a speech therapist. That's it. It's simple, and just from the premise you can already guess what happens in it.

Yet the movie takes such a simple, high-concept idea and executes it in a way that sucks you in. And that's all storytelling. Being a screenwriter is all about great storytelling. It's knowing how to maximize a scene to milk all you can from it. It's about building an engine and rewarding viewers and readers along the way. It's giving them just enough to keep them interested.

By taking this journey to becoming a screenwriter, there are little things like learning how to weave prose or how to hear dialogue that matter. But ultimately, the most important thing is storytelling and increasing your storytelling abilities.

What's a Treatment?

You already have an idea of what to write and you know who your story is about. So now it's time to finally start writing, right? No. Simply having an idea of what you want to write about isn't good enough. You need to know exactly where the story is going before you sit down to write. How do you do that? With structure!

Before I define "structure," let me throw out another buzzword: plot. Plot is all the junk that happens in your story. Structure, then, is the order in which the junk happens. If you think of your story as a house, then the structure is the foundation. It's what holds the house up.

A treatment is a one-page summary of your entire story. That might sound intimidating, but don't forget that we've already written a pitch and created a character arc for your protagonist, so at this point, all we really need to do is flesh them out. But before we do so, we need to talk about the dreaded THREE-ACT STRUCTURE…dun dun dun!

The Three-Act Structure

The first thing to know about the three-act structure is that there is no such thing as a three-act structure. It's actually four acts, but don't worry about that yet. For now we are going to keep it simple and embrace the myth of the three-act structure.

The three-act structure supposedly dates back to Greek times, though I personally have never read any three-act Greek plays. You're more likely to recognize it from movies, and it's become such a common storytelling tool that it also regularly appears in comic books and novels.

When using a three-act structure, Act I is used to build your world. In it your audience meets the protagonist and is exposed to their flaws. They learn about the world or environment the protagonist lives in and they get to see the kind of relationships your character has with other people.

Act II is the meat of your story. Everything is already set up, which means that Act II gets to focus on creating conflict. This whole section is nothing but the protagonist getting into more and more trouble, all of which has to in some way be their own fault. It should end with the protagonist at rock bottom.

Act III is where everything comes together. The protagonist rises from their lowest point, learns from their mistakes and fixes everything.

To sum it up, Act I is your beginning, Act II is your middle and Act III is your end.

Applying the three-act structure to "Iron Man," it breaks down like this:

- Act I — We meet Tony, learn that he is an arrogant, selfish jerk, and then watch as he is captured by a terrorist. To free himself, he creates the ultimate weapon and escapes.
- Act II — Inspired by his exploits, Tony decides to create Iron Man and spends all of Act II becoming Iron Man. He builds his new suit and then learns how to use it. The act ends with Tony being too cocky and losing everything.
- Act III — Tony rises from the ashes and redeems his flaw by

putting others first. He saves the day and becomes a hero.

The structure works for nonaction movies too. Let's look at the romantic comedy "Hitch."

- Act I — Will Smith is a cocky jerk who doesn't believe in love. He is hired to help a schlub score his dream chick, and along the way he meets the love of his life.
- Act II — Everything is going great. After training his client, Will Smith's own relationship grows and he is happy until his flaw comes out and everything is ruined.
- Act III — Will Smith overcomes his flaw and helps Kevin James get the girl, while at the same time sucking it up and admitting his feelings for the love of his life.

As you can see, in its simplest form the three-act structure isn't hard to master. So let's apply it to "Virgin Dad."

- Act I — We meet Eugene. We learn what his life is like and what his flaws are. We also learn that he's up for the big $20 million contract. Then his daughter Meta shows up and, after the initial "is she my daughter or isn't she my daughter" internal debate, he decides to take her in.
- Act II — Meta and Eugene's first conflict takes place. Just when they start to fall into a routine and become a family unit, Eugene screws it up and loses Meta.
- Act III — Realizing his mistake, Eugene sets out to make amends. He overcomes his flaws and fixes his life.

See? Easy as pie!

Writing the Treatment

When writing your treatment, you don't include backstory or anything extra. You start it where your story starts, giving a prose description of what it's about. In many ways, you can consider it a more fleshed-out version of your pitch that incorporates your character's arc. It may not seem important, but it really helps with figuring out the beginning, middle and ending of your story.

Basically, a one-page treatment should introduce your key characters and your story's who, what, when, where and why as follows:

- Act 1 in one to two paragraphs, including your protagonist's main flaw and conflicts.
- Act 2 in two paragraphs, dramatizing how the conflicts introduced in Act 1 lead to a crisis in which your protagonist fails to overcome their flaw and screws everything up.
- Act 3 in one to two paragraphs, dramatizing the final conflict and resolution.

Keep in mind that there are no set rules with treatments. There is a lot of wiggle room, and it's really about figuring out what works best for you. The main idea is that you turn your pitch and character arc into a one-page description of your entire story, using the three-act structure as a guidepost.

If you still aren't sure what to write, think of a treatment as an explanation of how readers will experience your story. It's important to use active voice and to avoid vague or hyperbolic phrases. You want your reader to be able to visualize your story, so it might even help to write it in present tense. It is a creative assignment, so make sure your treatment feels alive and not merely a cold presentation of the facts.

This is what a treatment for "Virgin Dad" would look like:

Middle-age virgin and nerd Eugene Baker is about to score a career-saving contract for $20 million. All he has to do is present his

AI robotics program to the Department of Defense, which will also secure his nod for a Nobel Prize. But on the day he is to give his presentation, Meta, a 12-year-old girl claiming to be his test-tube daughter, arrives.

After begging for a second chance to meet with the DoD representative, Eugene has to balance the life of a workaholic scientist with that of a new father. From Girl Scouts and talent shows to lab coats and science fairs, he has to do it all with the fate of his career on the line.

Through a few rough patches, Eugene makes it work. Although he will never be named Father of the Year, he manages to do what he has to. But when his contract with the government is outbid, the house of cards crumbles and Eugene puts his career first, ignoring Meta. Feeling hurt and scorned, Meta ruins the bid with the DoD.

Jobless and familyless, Eugene is forced to realize that his work isn't what really matters. The only thing that matters in life is family, and with some quick-thinking skill he manages to make amends with his daughter at her school science fair.

Several fun things arose when I wrote this treatment. For instance, the science fair just popped into my head when thinking about school activities for Meta to be involved with. Because setups and payoffs are important, the science fair is a great thing to show up at the start of Act II and something to build up to for Act III.

Of course the treatment should be cleaned up a bit, but I wanted to keep it basic so you guys could see what a rough one looks like. Going back and analyzing it, there are key things that you should note:

The whole treatment is about Eugene's character arc: He has a flaw. He tries to overcome the flaw. It looks like he will overcome the flaw. He fails and his life is ruined. Learning from his mistake, he rises from his failure and does whatever it takes to fix his life.

Since I have the main bits of the treatment done, now I'll go back and flesh it out more. I want to be more specific about the events that will happen, and I want to add more of Meta because she's really important to the story, and right now the treatment makes no real mention of her wants or goals. So a rewrite of it would look like this:

Virgin and Doctor of Science Eugene Baker has created an almost perfect artificial intelligence and is about to sell it to the Department of Defense for $20 million. Not only will it define his legacy as a scientist, but it also will save his research department from being cut due to his university's dwindling budget. On the day he is supposed to give his presentation to the DoD, he gets an unexpected visitor: Meta, a 12-year-old girl claiming to be his test-tube daughter.

After missing his important meeting to deal with Meta, Eugene uses his lab to run a maternity test and discovers that Meta is in fact his daughter. And if he doesn't take her in, she will end up in a run-down community home.

After taking Meta in, Eugene convinces the DoD to reschedule his meeting for three weeks later — that's three more weeks he has to prove his findings and three weeks of having to juggle his work with being a father.

Trying to keep Meta out of his hair so that he can work, Eugene enrolls her in every activity that he can think of, from Girl Scouts to soccer to the school's science fair. The whole time Meta begrudgingly goes along with it, desperately wanting to find her own place, but her lack of trust constantly prevents her from truly fitting in anywhere.

In the days leading up to the science fair, everything is clicking into place and, for a brief moment, Meta and Eugene exist as a true family unit. But it all crumbles to dust when Eugene cannibalizes Meta's science fair project for his meeting with the Department of Defense.

Not only does Eugene scorn his daughter, but his guilt over it distracts him from his work and he blows his contract with the DoD, causing him to lose his job and the legacy he was trying to build for himself in the field of science.

Jobless, alone and miserable, Eugene realizes the only thing that mattered in his life and made him truly happy was the brief time he and Meta were a real family. Setting out to fix his mistakes, Eugene rebuilds Meta's science project, winning back the affection of his daughter as well as proving to her that she can, in fact, trust him.

It's not the most beautiful prose I've ever read, but I'll tell you what — it feels like a real story! It's not perfect, but that's OK, because I'll refine it even more in the next few chapters.

Assignment Time

Write a one-page treatment for your screenplay.

Your treatment should be a nice blend of your pitch, your protagonist's wants, your protagonist's character arc and the three-act structure. If any of those things are missing, go back and rewrite. And make sure you get specific in your treatment. When I started writing mine, I didn't know about the science fair or that it would be the thing that causes everything to fall apart at the end of Act II. So if you are stuck, make sure you take the time to really think about those kinds of events that will populate the structure of your story.

CHAPTER SIX

The Beat Sheet

I don't believe in writer's block. I think writer's block is an excuse for bad planning. It's when a writer writes themselves into a hole and doesn't know where to take things. So how do we prevent that from happening to you? We plan. Then we plan some more. Then we plan even more. That way, when it's time for you to finally sit down and write, you'll have a road mapped out for you. Sure, you can step off of it and check out the scenery or stop to see The World's Largest Pie, but with that road you'll never be lost.

I have an uncanny sense of direction, and as a result I've only been lost once in my life. I was in my late 20s and it was when I first got into hiking and being healthy. I live on the Eastern Shore of Maryland, basically that bit of land between the Chesapeake Bay and the Atlantic Ocean. Everything there is just about sea level. Hills and big woodland forests are rare, so I was really excited when I discovered the Pocomoke River State Park. It had a lot of amazing reviews online and photos of the hiking trails looked great.

I got to the park. I parked and I found the hiking trail. It was nothing fancy — just an overgrown old dirt road. I picked a four-mile loop and headed out onto it.

I got maybe 50 feet onto the trail when I realized something was wrong. I hit a spiderweb that went from above my head to my ankles. It was disgusting! But there was a pride issue at hand. I was so excited to be going on the hike and didn't want to wuss out. I wanted to prove to myself that I could do it. So I kept on walking.

Within minutes I hit another spiderweb, but my stubbornness started to build. I picked up a dead tree branch and waved it in front of me as I walked. This system worked fairly well. Sure, my arm grew tired pretty darn fast, but it kept the spiderwebs out of my face.

About half a mile into the walk, I discovered why there were so many spiderwebs. The hiking trail was basically a dirt road through a marsh swamp. On each side of the road were standing water and knobby cypress knees. In the heat of June, there were misquotes everywhere.

Of course I was a newbie to the whole exercise thing. Nowadays when I go hiking, I always have my CamelBak backpack that's loaded with gear and provisions. Now I would just whip out some DEET insect repellent or a hat with a net. But the younger me was naive, and the only thing I could think to do was use my free hand and spin it in front of my face to keep the bugs from getting in my nose, mouth and eyes. It didn't work.

There were three main types of bugs out there. There were these evil horseflies that would leave massive welts where they bit me. Then there were the misquotes, which would land daintily but leave me stinging. Finally there were the gnats, which swarmed around me in dense clouds.

So there I was waving my dead branch in front of me with one hand and swatting away bugs with the other hand when I stumbled upon a ball of snakes. I kid you not — multiple snakes wound together in a creepy ball thingy. I've since learned that it was mating season, and that's why the snakes were there. I'm generally not one to be scared of snakes, but it was the last straw. I saw through the woods a road ahead and I bolted full speed for it. It was so nice to be on sunlit asphalt again and away from the all the disgusting biting things!

I had a vague idea what road I was on when I emerged, but I wasn't 100 percent sure. When I left the hiking trial I had seen a two-mile marker, which meant I could either go back into the woods and face two more miles of hell or I could follow the road around the park and hope it would take me back to the entrance. I chose the road.

Some of you are probably asking, "Why didn't you use your cell phone?" I tried. I was in the middle of nowhere, so my GPS wasn't working. So I picked a direction and started walking. And I walked. And I walked some more. Then I walked some more. After about two hours, I started to get really worried.

Finally I hit a road I recognized and nearly panicked when I realized I had gone the wrong way. I later learned I was a good eight miles away from my car.

I had two options. I could walk to the nearest town, which was maybe a mile, or I could turn around. My feet were blistered and bleeding. I was sweating more than I ever had in my life. I knew that if I went to town, someone would take pity on me and take me back to my car.

Again, you are probably wondering why didn't I call for help. Well, my mom was at work and my dad was disabled and couldn't drive. My one best friend was out of town and my other best friend was home with his son while his wife was out shopping, and since he didn't have the car seat, he couldn't go anywhere. I didn't have a girlfriend at the time, so I couldn't call her. I did try calling a taxi, but there were no local taxis and it would've cost me over $100 for one to come get me. So that's why I chose to walk to Snow Hill, Md.

Snow Hill is actually a really cute town. It's the county seat, so thanks to the courthouse, the downtown businesses have been able to stay alive and kicking. Of course, in the state I was in, I couldn't really appreciate it.

I managed to find a police officer, but he said he couldn't help because he was late for court. But then I saw a woman in a Department of Natural Resources shirt leaving the courthouse. I approached her and she said she was going to the Pocomoke River State Park and would be more than happy to take me there. As she drove, I told her my tale and she really enjoyed it — maybe a little too much.

When we finally got to the state park, I immediately knew something was wrong. I didn't recognize a single thing. I told the DNR woman and she laughed really hard. Apparently the state park has two locations — one on each side of the river — and she had brought me to wrong side. To make matters worse, she had an important meeting and couldn't take me to the other side of the river because driving there would take over 30 minutes. She did say that she could take me to my car when her meeting was over in three hours. Or, she said, if I was in a hurry, I could always rent a kayak and row across the river.

Since I was exhausted and in desperate need of a shower, I chose the kayak. The rental cost only $10, and wanting to shower has always been amazing motivation for me.

Kayaking wasn't as easy as I thought it would be. The biggest problem is that I had only done it once before in my life, and the DNR woman had made it sound like all I needed to do was paddle across a river. That was not accurate. The east side of the park is several miles north of the west side of the park, so I actually had to paddle downriver against the current.

It took me a lot longer than I thought it would, but it was honestly the most uneventful part of my day. In fact, it was really nice and peaceful. Until I tipped the kayak.

I managed to get the kayak back to shore — kind of. You see, this section of the river was completely surrounded by forest and swamps. There was no actual shore or beach for me to flip the kayak on. Then, when I got closer to the forest, the water turned into thick, stinky mud, and I swear I felt stuff moving under it.

So I managed to flip the kayak and get some of the water out, but there was no way for me to get back into it. So I ended up swimming several miles, tugging it along behind me. The good thing was that even filled with water it floated, so I was able to stop and take breaks. The bad news is that the water turned the 40-pound kayak into a several-hundred-pound kayak. So by the time I finally arrived at Milburn Landing on the west side of the park, I was exhausted. I barely managed to crawl onto shore.

My next problem was that there was no place for me to return the kayak. I had assumed I could just take the kayak to the rental place on the west side of the river. Nope. I had to return it to where I rented it from. I didn't have any straps to put it on top of my car, but I was able to fit it inside. See, I've been saying "car" this whole time, but really I owned a minivan. I've always been a soccer mom on the inside. And luckily for me it was only a 10-foot kayak, so it fit inside my van.

The bad news — and haven't you figured out that this day was all bad news? — is that the kayak wasn't fully in the van when I slammed the rear hatch closed. The kayak shot forward and cracked my windshield, and I was lucky the windshield didn't outright shatter.

I crawled into my car and started making the 30-minute drive back to Shad Landing on the east side of the park. Within a mile I got pulled over for having a cracked windshield. And lo and behold, do you know who it was? The cop who had refused to help me earlier in town! He looked at me and said, "What the hell happened to you?" I told him to go fluff himself, but I didn't use the word "fluff." I got a ticket for having a cracked windshield.

From there it was a simple matter of returning the kayak, and then I was finally able to make the 45-minute drive home. I had never been so exhausted than I was that day, nor have I ever been as completely lost as I was multiple times that day. So the point of all of this? Being lost sucks. And some of this story will come in handy because it's all about the structure of storytelling!

Story Beats

Screenwriters live and die by structure. It's just how Hollywood works. Most movies have a basic structure and the following is how it breaks down. (Note: most screenplays are 100 to 120 pages.)

ACT I

Opening – This is an attention-grabbing scene that sucks in the viewer and sets up the premise of the movie. For example, if you are doing an action movie, then this scene will be a big action sequence.

Page 3 – By the third page of a screenplay, we should've met the character and know the central question in the movie. It can be simple or complex. In a romantic comedy, it might be "Will John ever get a girlfriend?" And to set it up, you may have dialogue of him whining or complaining about not having a girlfriend. Or maybe he's a player, and instead of whining he's claiming he would never settle down no matter what.

Pages 3 to 10 – This is where you get to know your main character: their personality, their flaws, etc. This is where you set up their story arc and show how they've grown and changed over the course of the story.

Page 10 – The catalyst for the story should happen by this point. It does not always have to be a result of the protagonist's actions, but take care not to let your main character become too passive. So in a romantic comedy, this might be the first scene in which the boy meets the girl. In an action movie, this might be where the main character's daughter gets kidnapped, which spurs him into action.

Page 30 – Your midpoint scene should happen somewhere between pages 20 and 30, depending on the genre in which you are writing. It's one of the most important scenes in your story. Based on everything that has happened, your character needs to commit to the journey in front of them. So in a romantic comedy, this might be when the boy and the girl start dating. In an action movie, it might be when the father learns that a terrorist has captured his daughter but will let her go if he kills a senator.

The Act I endpoint scene is all about spinning the story in a new direction while making sure you embrace your character's flaws, because ultimately the character will fail at their task or journey because of those flaws.

ACT II

First half (Page 30) – Act II is a beast. It's total hell. Personally, it's what I hate about writing a screenplay more than anything else. Instead of thinking of it as 60 solid pages, it's best to break it in half. So in a romantic comedy, the first half of Act II is the characters dating. Or in something like "Iron Man," it's Tony building the suit and learning how to use it.

Midpoint (Page 60) – The midpoint scene is a recommitment to the goal or task in the end scene of Act I. So in a romantic comedy, maybe it's the characters taking things a step forward. They are past the wooing stage and are now a couple. Or in "Iron Man," it's Tony finishing his suit and deciding to use it to be a hero. It's important to once again have the character embrace their flaw.

Turning point (Page 90) – Things go to hell. Everything goes wrong because of the main character's flaw. So in a romantic comedy, it's when the girl dumps the guy because he's immature. Or if it's an action movie, maybe it's when the father assassinates the senator and is arrested. In a fantasy-type piece, it's when the heroes fail to stop the villain from destroying the world and the big bad guy starts wrecking things.

ACT III

Rock bottom – You need to hurt your protagonist. You need to utterly break them. There are three main things you need to do: take away their family, take away their job or career (their career could be becoming a hero and saving the world; it doesn't have to be a "job" job) and take away their love. It's a deadly trifecta.

Epiphany moment – This is the part in "House" when someone says something random and he suddenly solves the case. He gets that look in his eyes and just knows the answer. In a movie, this moment is like that but not as dramatic. It's when the character is at rock bottom and something happens to make them realize their flaws for the first time. They realize what they've been doing wrong and that they need to fix it.

Amends – This is when the main character makes up with his supporting cast. So in the romantic comedy in which the guy lost the girl and then pushed his friends away, this is when the guy would apologize to his friends and then ask for their help to get the girl back.

Climax – This is the most dramatic point, the culmination of your story.

Final temptation – This is a very important moment that a lot of people miss. Your character started out on a journey. They had a flaw. Everything went wrong because of that flaw. They learned their lesson and then started to fix things. The final temptation is the one last time your antagonist tempts your protagonist into re-embracing their character flaw. If the point of your story is for your main character to grow, then have them do the right thing. If you are doing an antihero story or have a darker theme, then maybe your character fails and they re-embrace their flaw. It doesn't matter which way you go; just make sure you have that moment.

Epilogue – This is your end scene. There is normally a flashback or reference to the very first scene of the movie. It is often referred to as a "bookend."

If you want homework, pop in some of your favorite movies and watch the first 30 minutes. "Back to the Future"; any "Star Wars," "Indiana Jones," "Iron Man" or "Aliens" installment; "Sweet Home Alabama"; "Hitch"; "Men in Black" — whatever. As long as it's a mainstream studio film, you'll be able to see the structure. For example, here is the Act I breakdown of "The Lord of the Rings: The Fellowship of the Ring."

Opening – Gladriel explains the epic history of the ring. This attention-grabbing scene sets up the Middle-earth world and the overall conflict.
Our hero – We meet Frodo Baggins and Gandalf the Grey.
The Hobbit life – We see what life in the Shire is like for our main Hobbit cast members.
The ring – We are introduced to the ring and witness the power it has over Bilbo.
Catalyst scene – Bilbo fakes his death and Frodo takes up the ring.
Bad guys – We see Gandalf visit the White Tower. We see the Nine Riders ride. We see Frodo and Sam try to lead their normal lives, but something isn't right.
 Act I end point – The Nine Riders reach the Shire and as a result Frodo, Sam, Merry and Pippin start their journey.

A problem with story beats is that they can feel forced. In a way, as a writer you are playing god, and as an omnipotent entity you are bossing around your protagonist, telling them what to do. If this is not done right, your protagonist becomes passive and weak.

What do I mean by "passive"? Your character and the decisions your character makes have to drive the story forward. You want things to happen because your character causes them to happen. If things happen to your character and all they are doing is reacting, that's passive and weak.

My hiking story is a perfect example. Every damn thing that happened to me on that day was my fault. Every time I made a decision, I got myself into more trouble and I had no one to blame but myself. When you are figuring out the beats of your story, you need to make sure the events happen in an organic way that leaves your protagonist in charge.

Write Out Your Beats

The reason we wrote a treatment in the last chapter is that it will be your guidepost for writing your beat sheet in this chapter. For 90 percent of the stuff you need, you'll turn to the treatment for the answer. Let's look at the beat sheet for "Virgin Dad."

Opening – We open 12 years ago, when Eugene is still in college. He's at a sperm bank asking the teller to withdraw a previous deposit. She tells him she can't do that.

So why did I go with this for my opening scene? Since the movie is called "Virgin Dad," right away we need to answer how Eugene can be both a virgin and a father. Plus, uber-arrogant nerd Eugene at a sperm bank, trying to give them money to get back his sperm, is a hilarious concept. It will be a lot of fun to write and it will instantly define who he is as a character. It also will set up the tone of the movie. This is supposed to be a quirky comedy, so right off the bat I want to establish my sense of weird humor.

Page 3 – Eugene is in the lab finishing up his scientific coding so that he can present his work to the Department of Defense the next day.

This is an important scene because it sets up Eugene's main goals. On a superficial level, the whole movie will revolve around the question "Will Eugene get the $20 million?" So we need to set that up right away.

Pages 3 to 10 – We see Eugene at the lab getting ready for his meeting with the DoD, and we see his home life. We will meet a coworker and his cousin.

Eugene's flaw is that work is the only thing that truly matters to him. How do we show that? Visually we can do that by showing him spending more time at work and that his home appears unlived in and cold. But we also will introduce supporting cast members. I already know from my interview with Eugene that he has a cousin. She'll be one of our main supporting cast members, and she'll be the person who will prod him along, saying that family is what really matters.

Page 10 – This is where Meta shows up at Eugene's door, causing him to miss his meeting with the DoD.

The story is all about Eugene learning to be a dad and discovering the importance of family. Once we've established in the first few scenes that work is his priority, we have to introduce Meta so that we can start Eugene on the arc that will leave him changed at the end of the story.

Page 30 – In this scene, Eugene is faced with choosing whether he will in fact take in Meta and be her father or kick her to the curb and let her deal with foster care.

Depending on your screenplay, this scene could come earlier. Normally it's between pages 20 and 30, depending on the length of your story. But I have a feeling this will fall a little bit earlier in "Virgin Dad." This beat is what it is because it's the only scene that could possibly take place for the story to be compelling.

We already know that Act II of "Virgin Dad" is about Eugene being a father. But first he must accept the responsibility of being a dad. Just as Meta shows up in his life of her own accord, it has to be Eugene's choice to keep her for him to be an active character.

Midpoint – Eugene agrees to help Meta with her science fair project, confirming that even though his career is on the line, he is trying to be a father.

We know that the first half of Act II will be a bumpy journey for Meta and Eugene. So instead of Eugene giving up and calling it quits, this midpoint scene must be one in which he decides he's not going to give up yet.

Page 90 – Eugene destroys Meta's science fair project to use in his new presentation to the Department of Defense.

This bit is really important because it's Eugene giving in to his flaw and making a mistake. Even though he's spent the whole first part of the movie trying to be a dad, he just isn't ready to accept it. Instead he makes his career a bigger priority, destroying his home life to save his work life.

Rock bottom – This is the end for Eugene. He's lost his contract, he's lost his job, he's lost Meta. Everything sucks.

Rock bottom is the point where you hurt your character as much as possible. Why? Because as I stated several chapters ago, people can change, but generally only after going through some sort of mental or physical trauma. In this case I need to fully break Eugene on an emotional level so that he can grow and become a better person.

Epiphany moment – After seeing his cousin Chloey and her family interactions, Eugene realizes the errors of his ways and decides to fix his life.

I have yet to figure out what Chloey's wants or needs are. I won't really deal with fleshing out my supporting cast until after I've taken care of my leads. However, the supporting cast does need to serve a purpose. They need to somehow be important to your protagonist's growth and journey. In this case, Chloey is going to be Eugene's Jiminy Cricket. She'll be the beacon of light that inspires Eugene to do the right thing and embrace being a father.

Amends – Just in time for the science fair, Eugene will blow off a final meeting with the DoD and instead present Meta with a repaired project and fix things with her.

This one is pretty obvious. I stole it directly from my treatment. It's Eugene sacrificing his career to put Meta first.

Climax – The science fair will be judged and, after thinking for a moment that they will win the fair, Meta and Eugene lose.

Final temptation – The DoD will be at the science fair and love Meta's project. They will offer Eugene a boatload of money for it. He will turn down their offer, saying that it is his daughter's project and not his to do anything with.

Epilogue – I don't have an epilogue yet for "Virgin Dad," and that's OK. It's hard to come up with an idea for a scene like that when I haven't even written any of my characters yet, because it really needs to be a final wrap-up of the whole movie. Your epilogue needs to sum up the theme of your movie and really invoke a lot of emotion and payoff. So I'll deal with it later, once I've gotten to know my characters better.

Assignment Time

Figure out the following beats for your screenplay: Opening, Page 3, Page 3-10, Page 10 - catalyst, Act I turning point, Act II part I, Act II midpoint, Act II turning point, Rock Bottom, Epiphany moment, Amends, Climax, Final temptation, & Epilogue.

CHAPTER SEVEN

FIGURING OUT THE DETAILS

There is a great scene in "Galaxy Quest" in which a fanboy approaches a washed up sci-fi actor and asks him how in a specific episode a part of the ship worked when in another episode it worked in a different way. The scene pokes fun at fanboy- and fangirl-isms and is good for a laugh. However, what I've come to discover is that as silly as it was, those kinds of things actually happen.

I've been to multiple comic conventions and approached by readers who have specific questions about how things work in my comic book "Holiday Wars." They will cite things like, "In Volume 1, in Panel 3 of Page 46, the character said 'blah blah blah,' but then in Volume 2 we learned that XX actually works because of YZ. How can that be?"

Luckily for me, I did my research. I have pages upon pages of notes regarding the rules of the "Holiday Wars" universe. So far — fingers crossed — I've always had an answer for those kind of fans. It's something I didn't expect to happen, but when you have people who care as much as you do about the characters that you create and their world, those kinds of questions will come up. This is why before you sit down and actually write your story, you need to make sure you do your research.

Research Time

Now is the time to do it.

I don't know how spaceships work. I don't know how real ones work, nor do I know how they work in popular sci-fi universes like those of "Star Wars" or "Star Trek." Sure, I could throw around a lot of technobabble off the top of my head, but it would be meaningless.

For example, I could say that the ship moves faster than light because of the warp core. It bends dark matter and creates miniature wormholes that allow the ship to travel at an accelerated rate through the vast expanse of space.

Sure, it may sound smart, but the problem with the above description is that it's actually nothing but empty words. If I was to write a real story involving spaceships, I would need to take the time to figure out how they actually work in my story's universe. I would research both real science and well-known science fiction to create a world that my characters could play in.

Unfortunately, I can't really offer you any clues or guides to research. It's really just figuring out your world. For example, if you were writing a fantasy story, you would need to sit down and create a geographic map and diagram how the government works. If there is magic, you need to know the rules of magic. If you are writing a science-fiction story, then you most likely need to figure out the way spaceships work and the fake science behind them.

The idea is that this is the ideal time to figure out your world so that when you go to play in it, you don't get distracted with the details.

When you are deeply into writing a scene about a wizard using a fireball, you need to know ahead of time how he summons the magic to do that. If you don't, you'll have to stop writing and waste time figuring that out on the fly.

The problem with research, however, is that you can get stuck in it. I have students who will waste weeks and weeks researching, and it ends up becoming this horrible time sink — nothing but a way to procrastinate from moving forward.

You really need to know yourself and your level of willpower when doing research. You have to have ability to say to yourself, "I've got this all figured out, and I'm good."

The other thing to keep in mind when researching is that you can look to places other than just Wikipedia or other websites. Maybe it's because I spent time as a news reporter, but I honestly get more from talking to people than I do from the Internet. If I were writing a courtroom drama and I didn't already have a law degree, I'd hire a lawyer as a consultant and spend a really long lunch picking their brain. If you are short on cash, another great resource is professors at your local college. Most of the time, offering a free lunch will get you really far.

My Research

Looking at "Virgin Dad," there is a lot of important stuff I need to know before I can even write an outline. For example, I don't know about adoption laws or things like that for Washington, D.C., where I want to set my story. Although I know how college hierarchies and politics work, I've never worked at a research school or a department in which research is important. So I need to figure out how that works. I also know absolutely nothing about the Department of Defense. I need to figure out how it works and if it really would buy some sort of cool new scientific artificial intelligence. If it wouldn't, then I need to find some other entity such as a mega-corporation that will serve the same roll.

I won't bother you with all the details of my research, but here are my main results and how they affect the story I've already planned out:

Eugene made a donation to a sperm bank when he was in college. An employee at the bank illegally used it to inseminate herself. She had a child and listed Eugene on the birth certificate out of guilt. Years later, the mom dies and Meta is brought to Eugene because he is the legal and biological father, even though he had no idea.

Eugene works at TimeBox, a research facility in the corridor outside of Washington, D.C. The project Eugene has been working on is part of a $20 million contract that will fall through completely if he doesn't finish coding the AI.

Inspired by her father, Meta creates a board game for a science project that uses functioning AI. At the end of Act II, when Eugene's own research project is broken, he destroys Meta's science project for the parts.

So why the details about the donation? Well, I discovered that sperm donors sign papers giving up their legal rights, which means if Eugene was just an everyday sperm donor, there would be legal issues and social services involvement and that kind of stuff. The idea is to achieve what I want — getting Meta to live with him — without having to spend scene after scene on exposition that takes up too much space.

I dropped the ideas of Eugene working for a university and pursuing a DoD contract because it was just too much to deal with.

They were conflicting for space. There is only so much room in a screenplay, and it was becoming difficult to force both things to fit. Instead, it made much more sense to combine the environments into one entity (a high-tech company on par with government research) with one set of supporting characters.

Then the issue with Meta and the board game was just me figuring out what I wanted her to do. I knew I wanted gaming somehow involved because games are social by their nature. They're about people sitting around together having fun, so it fit into the "Virgin Dad" themes of social interaction and human connection. And although I'm not a gamer, I've always been fascinated by European-style games and all those fancy phrases gamers use. So I thought it might be fun to explore that world some through this screenplay.

I even went the extra mile. Not only did I talk to a few designers I know in the board game industry, but I also sat down and sketched out a board and created a whole game. It's called "Butterfly Storm." It's a tower defense game in which radioactive butterflies attack a suburban house, and it's up to a mom, dad, brother and sister to defend their home.

I know it's really specific — I even made a board and cards and wrote rules and all that stuff — but since Meta creating her game is a key element in my story, I wanted it to fit thematically into the arc of the whole movie and the theme of my story. That's why it's a game in which family members have to band together
cooperatively instead of a competitive one. Either you win together or you lose together.

I also watched a lot of YouTube videos for Meta. That might sound odd, but there is a huge culture of exhibitionism among the current younger generation, and YouTube is one of their most popular outlets. Tweens and teens aren't weirder than those of us who are older, it's just that technology has made it so easy to share your life. Anyone can now pull out a smartphone and start streaming live to the Internet. Since I want Meta to tap into that culture, I did extra research to try and figure out *why* YouTubers do what they do. Ultimately, I now have a much clearer idea of who Meta is.

Supporting Cast

It's time to think about your supporting cast. There are no magic rules or real tips I can give you. This is something you'll need to figure out on your own based on the story you are telling. You may need only two supporting cast members, or you may need six.

When creating your supporting cast, think about their relationships with your protagonist and antagonist. Your protagonist will act differently around different people. That's one reason it's nice to have a supporting cast, because it allows you to show your character's different traits and assets. For example, think about how you act around your mom. Is it different from or exactly the same as you act when you're around your friends?

The only thing to remember is that each supporting cast member needs to serve a purpose. If they don't, then get rid of them. They also need to have their own mini-stories. In their own minds, the supporting cast members are the stars of their own movies, so make sure you give them almost mini-story arcs.

In the case of "Virgin Dad," we have several worlds we need to populate. There is Eugene's work life, there is his home life, and then there is Meta and whoever she interacts with at school or whatever else we decide to do with her.

"Virgin Dad" supporting cast:

- Chloey, Eugene's cousin — She's Eugene's moral compass. I know she'll be dealing with some sort of personal issue. Maybe she's going through a divorce or can't get pregnant or something along those lines. Whatever it is, it will only be subtly hinted at.
- Zax, Chloey's kid — We'll make him crazy. Not literally, but hyper and weird. His role will be to show that Chloey is a good parent in contrast to Eugene.
- Bart, Eugene's coworker — He's the opposite of Eugene. He's not as smart, but he knows people and is great at playing the system. He wants Eugene to fail and get fired. He's going to be around to pressure Eugene and help him mess up. Whereas Chloey is the angel on Eugene's shoulder, Bart will be the devil.
- Francine, Eugene's boss — She's a cold, cold person. Think of her as completely lacking empathy, someone who functions based on logic and money alone.
- Johanna, Meta's science teacher — If we were doing a more cheeseball movie, she would be a potential love interest for Eugene. But this isn't that kind of movie. Instead she will be the voice of reason in Meta's world.

I may not use all of these characters when I start writing, and I may even come up with new supporting cast members depending on how the script changes when I start writing. This is just a guidepost.

Luckily for me, I've done this a few times and I can wing it. If you are feeling nervous about your supporting cast members, then redo the assignment in Chapter 3, but focus on your supporting cast instead of your protagonist and antagonist.

Assignment Time

Do whatever research you need to write your screenplay. Also take the time to flesh out your supporting cast members.

CHAPTER EIGHT

SCENE OUTLINE

Theoretically, if you are a tough go-getter, you might have read the first seven chapters of this book in one sitting. You might even have done all the assignments in one sitting. It would be a really long sitting, but it's doable. Either way, now is the time to hit the pause button.

If you really want to make it through your first screenplay, you need to slow down. In many ways, ideas are like fine wine. Sure, an idea you've just come up with can get the job done, but chances are if you let it ferment in your brain for a while, something even better and more complex might come out the other side.

Screenwriting really is all about planning. It's prewriting. This chapter and the assignments in this chapter are going to kick your butt, and for them to do that, you can't blow through them. You need to read the chapter. Let it sink in. Do the assignment. Let it sink in some more. Then come back to it after a few days. The choices you make at this stage are really important. So if it takes you a week or more to figure out everything in this next chapter, don't feel bad. That's how this whole process works.

I normally come up with an idea for a story months or even years before I sit down to write it. It just depends how busy I am and how many other projects I have on my plate. Once I do start the planning process, I could be in that stage for several weeks, and I'm someone who knows what he's doing. I've worked with screenwriters and have been taught by them, and it's the same thing for them. Planning can take awhile, and that's OK. It's better to take the time now to let ideas brew and figure them out, rather than getting into the middle of your script and realizing, "Oh crap, this does not work."

Outlining

Now that you have your beat sheet, we can get to the brunt of the whole screenwriting process: outlining! This is where structure really matters, and it's one of my favorite parts of the writing process. This entire step could take you days if not weeks, so don't feel bummed out if everything doesn't just click into place.

Outlining gives us a road map of where we are going with our stories. Keep in mind that every scene in your screenplay must do one of two things: move the plot forward or reveal character. Every scene needs to have a purpose, a reason for being in your story. Otherwise it's a waste of space.

Take your beat sheet and fill in the scenes for all of the beats, then logically, almost like playing a story version of connect the dots, determine what scenes are missing to get your characters from point A to point B.

Let's look at "Virgin Dad." The beats for Act I would look something like this:
- Sperm bank withdrawal
- Eugene's life
- Meta arrives
- Eugene decides to be a father

That span between pages 3 and 10 is all about Eugene's life. So we already know that it will be multiple scenes, because you'd never want a seven-page scene. So what happens there? Remember, we need to use that space to set up what Eugene's life is like before Meta arrives. What assets of his life should we highlight?

There is Eugene at work, Eugene with family (his cousin) and Eugene at home. We want to experience him in all three environments so that we can get to know him better as a character. So my scene breakdown for the first 10 pages of Act I would look like this:

Sperm Bank Withdrawal

What happens: Eugene goes to the bank to try and withdraw a sperm donation he previously made.

Character reveal: This is our first introduction to Eugene, and it is a great place to show how he has problems with social norms.

Plot point: This sets up how he can be both a virgin and a father.

Eugene at TimeBox

What happens: Eugene is doing an AI experiment with his coworker Bart watching. It doesn't go right.

Character reveal: We get to see a now more confident Eugene being good at science.

Character reveal: We get to see him awkwardly talking to Bart, who makes fun of him for being a virgin.

Plot point: We will set up here that there is a $20 million contract on the line, and if Eugene doesn't get things right, his company will lose it.

Eugene at Chloey's

What happens: Eugene arrives late for dinner at his cousin Chloey's.

Character reveal: We see that Eugene is horrible in every interaction with Chloey's son Zax.

Plot point: We learn that something happened to Eugene's family growing up and that, as a result, family means very little to him.

Home Alone

What happens: Eugene spends all night working at home until he falls asleep in his living room.

Character reveal: We see that Eugene is a workaholic who lives a lonely, cold home life.

Plot point: We further set up the science and AI system that will become important in both Meta's science project and Eugene's failed experiment at the end of Act II.

Surprise!

What happens: The lawyer delivers Meta, calling her Eugene's daughter.

Plot point: We and Eugene learn that he is a father.

Character reveal: Eugene does not want to be a father, nor does he want the responsibility that comes with it.

Although the rule is that every scene must have either plot movement or character reveals, it's best to try to squeeze both into them. Part of being a screenwriter is being economical with your space. Ninety to 100 pages may sound like a lot, but it's ungodly easy filling up that white space, and once you do, it's hard as heck cutting bits out. The best way to combat that from the beginning is to make every scene matter.

How to Outline

There are lots of ways to outline. I'm old-fashioned. I pull out plain white computer paper and make a list of every scene with quick notes about why it matters.

If you are more of a visual person, you can always use note cards. The benefit of this method is that you can shuffle scenes around. The downside is that at the end of the day you can't forget structure, and a scene that you planned for the start of Act I would never work in Act II.

There also are a lot of indexing and outlining applications for both smartphones and computers. In the past five years or so, mind maps have become popular, although they can sometimes be a pain to set up if you are using cheap software. So for now I say try them all to figure out what works best for you. Once you have your perfect outlining style, just make sure every scene has a point.

Assignment Time

Write a scene outline for your screenplay. Make sure every scene either moves the story forward or serves the character arcs you have planned out for your cast. Your ideal goal is for every scene to reveal both plot points and character development.

This is a beast of an assignment. It's one of the hardest assignments and one of the most important, so make sure you take this seriously and don't skimp on it. Don't be afraid to go back and adjust your pitch, character arcs or any other prep work you've done.

Doing a scene outline and really examining your story may cause you to shift everything around, and that's OK. That's why we are doing this. We want to make those kinds of tweaks and even overhauls now, before we waste time writing huge scenes that will end up being fully rewritten or even cut.

When you're done, you want to end up with a finished outline in whatever style works for you. Make sure you explain what happens in every scene and why that scene matters.

For comparison, flip back a few pages and look at the outline I used for Act I of "Virgin Dad."

CHAPTER NINE

SOFTWARE AND FORMAT

The first screenplay I ever read was "Dogma" by Kevin Smith. That's an odd thing to remember, but it was the '90s, I was in high school and the Internet was around but hadn't blown up yet.

When I got to college and fell in love with storytelling and screenwriting, I branched out. I started with screenplays of the classic movies and then worked my way through to some of my favorites.

I learned a lot just by reading. In fact, it's kind of crazy to say, "Hey, I'm going to write a screenplay, but I've never even seen one before." It reminds me of the hipsters in college who said they wanted a film degree and to make movies, but they didn't own TVs or computers because they felt everything was so watered down and bad it wasn't worth watching.

Writing is an art form, not a technical skill. That means no matter how much you learn, you'll never max out. One of the joys of being a writer is the constant evolution of your skills. Obviously you learn how to become a better writer by writing, and that's what you are doing by following the assignments in this book. But there are things you can learn by reading good writing that you could never learn in a classroom or from a textbook.

It's not just the great screenplays that can teach you. Once you understand basic structure and format, reading a really bad screenplay often can teach you more than a well-written one can. So outside of this book and its assignments, start reading as many screenplays as you have time to read.

Software

One of the most common questions I'm asked is what computer program to use. Here is a list of some of the more popular ones:
- Celtx (Mac & PC) – free at http://celtx.com
- Scripped (Mac & PC) – free at http://scripped.com
- Scrivener (Mac & PC) – $45 at http://www.literatureandlatte.com
- Final Draft (Mac & PC) – $249 at http://www.finaldraft.com
- Storyist Software (Mac) – $59 at http://www.storyist.com

I use Scrivener for my first draft and finish everything in Final Draft. I like Scrivener because it allows me to organize and structure my notes, but I wouldn't say it's a must-have. Same thing with Final Draft. Yes, Final Draft is the mac daddy of screenwriting software, but if you can't afford it, that's OK. There are a lot of other options, and to be honest, Final Draft is beginning to feel old and dated. So I recommend you try out several writing software options and pick what works best for you.

Elements of a Script

The majority of your script will consist of four elements: action lines, character names, dialogue and scene headings.

Scene Headings

These appear at the beginning of a new scene and tell us the scene's setting. They look like this:

INT. BAT CAVE – NIGHT

Or like this:

EXT. MADISON HIGH SCHOOL GYM – SUNRISE

Scene headings are always in all caps and made up of several elements. The first is always "INT." or "EXT." INT. stands for "interior," meaning the scene takes place indoors. EXT. stands for "exterior," meaning the scene takes place outside.

The next element is the location of your scene. In the above examples, the first location is the Bat Cave and in the second it's outside of a high school gym.

The final element is the time of day in which the scene takes place. The most common ones are simply "DAY" and "NIGHT." But sometimes you may need to be more specific, using "SUNRISE," "SUNSET," "EVENING," "CONTINUOUS" or even "LATER."

It is important to know not just how but when to use scene headings. You should do so at the start of each scene, by which I mean at every change of location. Using the gym scene example from above, let's say the scene starts with the characters inside of the gym and then they walk outside. That calls for a scene change. The only trick is that because there is no time change between these scenes, you would use "CONTINUOUS" as the time.

Action Lines

After you use a scene heading to establish your where and when, the next thing you need to include is action lines, which are basically your prose description of what is going on. Traditionally in screenwriting, your prose should be present tense, but with comic books it's whatever works best for you or your artist. We'll talk a little bit more about writing prose later.

Character Names

This is pretty obvious. It's giving the names of your characters whenever they speak. There are several variations. If a character is offscreen (o.s.) or you are doing a voice-over (v.o.), you can use tags after their names. Then, if you want to be more clear about how a piece of dialogue is being delivered, you can briefly describe the tone or specify whom your character is addressing, etc., in parentheticals.

The fourth element that will appear in your script is dialogue. It is indented underneath your character's name, and just about any script-writing program will do that for you automatically, so there really isn't much to talk about in terms of formatting.

Assignment Time

Pick a movie that's in the same genre as yours and read the screenplay. Make sure you don't pick a crappy movie. Pick a really good movie. Then, go to one of the many websites where you can find screenplays. Some are free, some are not — just try to make sure you are getting real screenplays and not just transcripts of movies. Transcripts are bad.

CHAPTER TEN

WRITING PROSE

It's no secret that I'm dyslexic. That means the hardest part for me when I write is the actual act of writing. It's also a reason why I've always gravitated to the screenplay format as opposed to novel writing. Don't get me wrong: I'm not saying screenwriting is easy. In fact, screenwriting is much harder than writing a novel. Yes, screenplays are shorter and filled with a lot of dialogue, but there are a lot more rules and structure involved in screenplays that novelists don't have to deal with.

Because screenplays are so dialogue heavy, many people think that the prose (action lines) isn't as important. But it's actually the other way around. Because there is so little of it, the prose needs to be that much more polished. It needs to be as concise as possible while still getting the job done.

So don't just skip over this chapter. Although writing prose can feel like a chore, it's just as important as every other element of your screenplay.

The thing to remember about scripting is that a screenplay is not a finished product. It is actually a collaborative medium, which means that a script isn't published when the writer is done writing it. It's used as a blueprint to build a movie.

The hardest thing about writing prose is that it takes time to get good at it. Back in my college days, I was told that it takes a person one million words before they start to get good at writing. It sounds silly but there is a lot of truth to it, because at the end of the day there is no trick to becoming a better writer. You simply have to practice (for a very long time).

That being said, here are some basic prose-writing tips that may help you out.

Show, Don't Tell

The first thing to remember with any script is that someone (sometimes you) is going to have to draw what you are describing. That means all your prose should be visual, because you are working in a visual medium. The easiest way to do this is to follow the "show, don't tell" rule. What do I mean by that? Let's look at the example below:

- Tell: Jane was sad.
- Show: Jane's eyes clenched tight as tears poured from them.

In both situations I'm getting the point across that Jane is sad, but I'm doing them in completely different ways. In the first, I'm flat-out telling you the information you need. In the second I'm showing you the information. See the difference?

You don't want to tell your reader what is going on. You want to show them. You want your reader to experience the events as they are happening. Plus, if you aren't drawing your storyboards or comic yourself, you want to give clear directions to your artist. If you simply said, "In Panel 1, make Jane sad," that's a very vague description. By showing and giving clear details, you'll make sure that the artist you are working with knows exactly what you mean.

Avoid Adverbs

An adverb is a modifier; it is used to describe an action. Words like "happily," "quickly" and "impatiently" are adverbs. They tend to end in "-ly." A simple rule to remember is not to use them. They are generally subjective terms that result in telling instead of showing. Also, they often get in the way of strong verbs. Look at the sentence below:

Tegan quickly walked to the exit.

"Quickly" is an adverb that is modifying the verb "walked." It's telling us that the pace she is using is faster than normal. Sure, it gets the idea across, but instead of using an adverb, we'd be much better off using a stronger verb. For example:

- Tegan ran to the exit.

OK, that was a little boring. What about this one?

- Tegan fled to the exit.

Or

- Tegan scurried to the exit.

A single strong verb can do ten times more for a sentence than five adverbs can.

Vary Sentence Length, Structure

There is no right length for a sentence, but it's a sign of a poor writer when all your sentence lengths and structures are the same. If you regularly use only short sentences, your writing will feel choppy. If you only use long sentences, your writing will feel like it drones on.

So when should you use either? A longer sentence works best as a way to offer more details, to focus on or probe an idea more thoroughly, or perhaps to present a powerful description. A short sentence gets to the point.

Avoid Passive Voice

Passive voice is a huge amateur writing error. It's when you use the "to be" verbs in unnecessary ways. Look at the sentence below:

- George was crying.

The to-be verb "was" in the sentence is completely unnecessary. It's an extra word that ends up weakening the verb. A much stronger sentence would be "George cried."

Here is a full list of to-be verbs:

- Present tense: I am, we are, you are, he/she/it is, they are
- Past tense: I was, we were, you were, he/she/it was, they were
- Perfect form (past participle): I have been, etc.
- Progressive form (present participle): I am being, etc.

Attune your eye to the to-be verbs and you'll see them everywhere. When in doubt, replace them with active, vivid, engaging verbs.

However, keep in mind that passive voice isn't *always* a bad thing. Sometimes it's best to use passive voice. As an example, in many ways "John is crying" feels more in the present than "John cries." And much of what happens in a screenplay should be about flow and feeling more than about grammar.

Yes, the prose should read nicely, but people often speak ungrammatically, so it's OK in dialogue for sure.

Assignment Time

Take a one-minute scene from a movie and turn it into prose writing. Make sure you don't cop out by picking a dialogue-heavy scene. Then get the screenplay for the movie and compare what you wrote to what the screenwriter wrote. Unless you picked a stinker of a film, chances are the prose in the screenplay is better than what you wrote. If so, look at the sentence structure, pacing and flow to get some ideas for how you could improve your first attempt.

CHAPTER ELEVEN

Writing Dialogue

Dialogue is strange. Anyone can learn to write dialogue, but at the same time you need to have a natural ear for it.

I learned how to write dialogue from online chatting. Back when I was a kid, we didn't have text messages or video chat, so instead you'd have a whole bunch of chat screens open on your computer as you were having three or four separate conversations with friends.

When participating in those chats, I realized that everyone has a voice, which is what we will talk about in this chapter. For example, I noticed that my best friend Sarah talked differently in the chat than my cousin Jessie did.

Looking back as a writer, I feel so stupid because it's like, "Uh, duh — of course people talk differently," but for me it was a revolutionary idea. The fact that different people use different words and that different people explain or say things in different ways was groundbreaking for me. After that moment, reading a book was shocking because I started to identify good writers by their fresh- or original-sounding characters.

Simply put, dialogue is words spoken between two or more characters. It must accomplish one of two things:
- Develop or reveal character
- Move the story forward

If your dialogue is ever doing something other than those two things, there is most likely a problem with it. You never want dialogue to be small talk or an exchange of pleasantries. It needs to have a point.

"Develop or reveal character" is a slightly vague phrase, so let's flesh out the concept real quick. You get to know a character by the things they say and do. If a character is a customer in a coffee shop who uses short, terse words toward the barista, it says something about them. If one character says "I love you" to another character, and the second character responds with "Uh-oh," that says something too.

I know that a moment ago I told you not to include small talk, but it's OK if the point of the small talk is to reveal character. Let's say you are writing a story about a socially awkward guy. Near the beginning of your story you may want to have a scene in which he partakes in awkward small talk to show just how unsocialized he is.

The same thing applies to moving the story forward. This can take the form of foreshadowing a major event that will happen near the end of the story or revealing information that your main character needs. It's a pretty wide-open rule, so don't feel too confined by it. Simply make sure there is a reason your characters are saying the things they do.

On top of that you need to remember our "show, don't tell" prose rule. It applies to dialogue too. You don't want a character to simply say how they are feeling. You want their feelings to show and their words to make their emotions clear. How do you do that and create dialogue that still works and sounds authentic? Like all aspects of writing, it simply takes time and practice. However, here are a few tips I've cobbled together that may help.

Listen to People Speak

If you want to be a better writer, then you should read a lot. If you want to write better dialogue, then you should listen to real people speaking. The next time you are in a cafe or at the grocery store, stop and listen to a conversation. Listen to how people form their sentences and the overall flow of the conversation. It sounds obvious, but it's important to write how people speak, and the only way you are going to learn that is by listening to people.

Dialogue Is Not Real

I know I just told you that dialogue should sound real, but you have to realize that dialogue isn't really real. When people speak, they throw in a lot of extra words and pauses. Or they randomly switch topics or they trail off during the middle of a sentence. In fact, I'm sure you've had a teacher or know someone else who constantly says "um" or "uh." Real-life conversation is clunky and reads awkwardly. So when you are writing dialogue, you need to cut out all the junk. The goal of dialogue isn't to mimic real speech; it's to deliver the good stuff while cutting out the crap.

For example, let's look at the fake conversation below:

"Hey, man, I think the FBI found Frank."
"I'll make sure he doesn't talk."
"Awesome, that sounds great."
"Yeah, well, I'll kill him before he has a chance."

"That's a shame. He makes these great blueberry muffins. Maybe you could get the recipe before you ... you know?"

"Actually, I already got it. It was his grandma's, and she was a friend of my Nana."

"Oh, sweet, I gotta get that from you."

"I'll give it to you on Saturday."

"That's right, we got that thing on Saturday."

"Yeah."

"What time is it?"

"Six."

"OK, yeah, I'll write that down."

"You better."

"Yeah, I suck at remembering stuff."

"Well, hey, I really gotta get back to making my origami."

"Oh, yeah. Sure. Sorry."

"No, it's cool. You didn't know."

"All right, I'll see you Saturday."

"Yeah, see you then."

"Bye."

"Bye."

If you put that in your story, people would probably stop reading right there. It's clunky. It's boring. It's too much information. A simple way to edit that whole conversation would be like this:

"The FBI found Frank."

"I'll make sure he doesn't talk."

Click (He hangs up the phone.)

That's it. Unless the recipe is some how integral to the plot, you don't need all the extra junk. So just remember that when you are writing out your real-sounding dialogue, it should sound real but not actually be real.

Dialogue Is Not Grammatical

People do not speak with perfect grammar. That means your dialogue shouldn't have perfect grammar.

Avoid Talking Heads

A talking-head scene is basically a super long scene in which people talk. Nothing really happens. There will be times when because of plot or whatever you will have to have a talking-head scene to deliver information. In those cases when you can't avoid it, then remember to give characters things to do. Have them get up and walk around or do something else physical to help break up the dialogue.

"On-The-Nose" Dialogue

One of the biggest mistakes a novice writer makes is using "on-the-nose" dialogue. This is when a character presents obvious-sounding information in their dialogue. For example, look at the scene below:

Daughter: At school today, Mary Claire threw a cup of yogurt at me and made fun of me in front of the whole cafeteria. It was bad and I cried.

Mom: Well, I will have to call your principal, Mr. Anders, and have a conversation with him about this.

Daughter: You already called him four times. Calling him again to tell him to stop the bullying will not do any good.

Mom: I am your mother and I love you. I want to do something. If I can't call, what else am I supposed to do?

Daughter: Nothing. You can't help me at all. Only I can help myself.

See what I mean by "on the nose?" It's extra exposition (which we will talk about in a minute) as well as a lot of telling instead of showing. A simple rewrite of this scene would be something like this:

Daughter: They did it again.

Mom: I'll speak to Mr. Anders.

Daughter: Don't bother.

Mom: Then what do you want me to do?

Daughter: Nothing.

Limit Exposition

Exposition is when a character shares chunks of necessary information to move the story forward. You'll end up using it at some point, which is OK, because it really is unavoidable. The key is to try to limit how or how much you use it. Spread information out through several scenes or try to deliver it in a more entertaining way. I'll talk about this more in a later chapter.

Limit Technobabble

Recall how in old "Star Trek" episodes someone would say something like, "But Captain, if we proceed to warp speed, the spanglier projector will ignite and cause a phase shift in the uberantium hull, which could lead to a rip in the space-time continuum." That's technobabble. Like exposition, if you are doing a genre story, it's sometimes unavoidable. The key is to keep it as short and to the point as possible.

Characters Have Voice

Every character should have a distinct voice, meaning that their dialogue shouldn't be interchangeable. For example, a 16-year-old girl doesn't talk the same as a 70-year-old man. Each would use different words and sentence structure.

It takes time to get better at creating distinct voices. The easiest way to practice is to listen to the voices of people around you who reflect your character's traits. If you are trying to write a teenager, then spend some time with a younger cousin or friend of the family. Pay attention to the words they use, how they emphasize them. If you are still having trouble, try asking yourself some of these questions:

- How old is the character?
- What do they do for a living?
- What is their education?
- Where are they from?
- What is their personality like?
- What is the relationship of the character to the person they are speaking to?

A good test for knowing if your characters have a strong voice is to simply cover up their names and see if you can still tell who is speaking. Keep in mind too that when I say "voice," I don't only mean an accent or dialect (in fact, the general rule of thumb is you should use as few accents as possible) or what the pitch or volume of their voice sounds like. A character's voice should reflect a speech pattern that reveals the answers to all the questions I posed above. It should reveal their personality, their attitude and their point of view.

As an extreme example, I'll use characters from my comic

"Holiday Wars," which is about characters that personify holidays. Because of the nature of the story, creating unique voices for most of the supporting cast was easy. Look at the following three characters:

- Ask A Stupid Question Day – She always ends what she is saying with a question, and nine out of 10 times it's either a stupid question or the answer is very obvious.
- Opposite Day – He always says the opposite of what he really means. So if he was in love with someone, he might look at them and say, "I hate your #%#%ing guts."
- Talk Like A Pirate Day – He talks not like a pirate, but in the horrible fake-pirate dialect that people use on the actual Talk Like A Pirate Day.

The above examples are extreme cases, but they clearly demonstrate my point. Characters need to sound different. They need to have unique voices.

Read it Aloud

Always, always, always read dialogue aloud to see if it sounds right. You might feel weird at first reading aloud at your computer, but it's a surefire way to see how chunky a character's dialogue is or isn't. Then you can always go the extra mile and actually do a read-through. Invite a few friends over, hand them your script and let them read the dialogue aloud.

Assignment Time

Go to a public place and sit somewhere where you can eavesdrop without looking creepy. A Starbucks or bookstore cafe would be ideal places. For at least five minutes, write down an entire conversation between two people. Take that conversation and break it down so that when in screenplay format, it fits onto a single page. You'll have to make smart choices about what things are meaningless and what things really matter.

CHAPTER TWELVE

What's in a Scene?

If your screenplay were a sidewalk, then each slab of concrete that formed the sidewalk would represent a single scene. Having your character move through it would consist of them walking from the start of your story through each scene until they reached the end.

It's a very linear process because time is linear. A person sits down and watches a movie from start to finish. You don't watch the middle of a movie, then rewind and watch the start, then jump ahead and watch the end. That's not to say that the scenes within the story couldn't jump around like that — lots of great movies use this technique. But the plot of a movie is told in a specific order chosen by the screenwriter for specific reasons, and scenes are the most basic measurement of that. Scenes make up your screenplay, and by focusing on them you'll be able to focus sharply on individual moments of time.

There are two main rules to remember when writing scenes:
- They must either move the story forward or develop character
- Enter late and leave early.

Rule one should be familiar by now. Like dialogue, every scene needs to have a purpose. It needs a reason for being in your story, otherwise it's a waste of space.

If you did a proper outline and stuck sort of close to it, then you shouldn't have too much of a problem making sure your scenes are relevant. When it comes time to rewrite (which we will talk about in a later chapter), you may shuffle things around and find that a scene that was once important is no longer necessary, but for the most part, planning should ensure that your scenes have a reason for existing.

Rule two needs a tad more explaining.

Enter Late, Leave Early

The idea behind this rule is that you come into a scene after stuff has already started to happen and you leave as soon as you get the important info. For example, let's say we have a dinner scene with two people out on a date. The events would look something like this:
- Arrive at restaurant
- Be seated by host
- Order drinks
- Order food
- Talk while waiting for food
- Get food
- Eat food
- Pay check
- Leave restaurant

Even if those events take place, you don't need to show all of them. Unless you are moving the story forward or developing character, doing so is boring. Depending on what interesting things are happening, you can skip most of the events on the list and cut right to the good stuff.

So when looking at your scenes, you really need to consider, "What's the latest moment I can start this scene?" and that's where you want to start it. Then you want to end the scene as soon as you get the important information across.

One of my favorite illustrations of "enter late, leave early" is an old story I heard back in college. Charley Chaplin was making a movie in the '40s. It was about a married couple who were having problems. There was an entire scene in which they got in an elevator, talked about their problems and ended the discussion with a fight. The scene supposedly lasted several minutes. It was too long, the dialogue was too on the nose and it simply didn't work.

To solve the problem, Chaplin cut all of the dialogue and gave the husband a hat to wear. Instead of having the couple arguing, they merely stood side by side. The elevator stops (it didn't before) and a woman walks on. As a sign of respect, the man takes off his hat and holds it. One floor later the woman gets off, and the husband puts his hat back on.

I have no idea if the story is true or not, but it's a good example of how editing down a scene and showing instead of telling can work better than long-winded talking-head scenes.

One final thing I want to mention — and I'm going to contradict myself — is that the "enter late and leave early" rule does not have to be set in stone. There will be times when you need to have a slow-paced scene to build up tension. This rule is really more of a guide developed for new writers because they have a habit of trying to put too much detail into a scene.

Assignment Time

Remember that outline you slaved over? Well, it's time for you to pick it up and re-examine it. I want you to go through your outline scene by scene and figure out the most optimal time to start and end each one.

When looking at your finished work, make sure you ask yourself if you entered late and left early. If you did, then you are golden. Just keep in mind, though, that unless you are writing a high-octane action piece, you will need to pace the story. So although "enter late and leave early" is a good rule, it's not a hard-and-fast one. It's simply meant to help you trim the fat. There will be times when, for pacing reasons, you don't want to enter late or leave early. Just make sure your script is sprinkled with a nice balance of both.

CHAPTER THIRTEEN

Making Time

The First Draft

You've done all the prep work. You've dabbled a little bit in prose, dialogue and the screenplay format. Now it's time for you to get dirty and actually start writing. But first we need to talk about the act of writing and the goal of the first draft.

Writing involves lots of rewriting, and chances are that after you finish your first draft, you'll end up going back and cutting anywhere from 30 percent to 60 percent of what you wrote. It's a pain in the butt and there is no way around it. By going through the process of writing the first draft, you get to know your characters and you discover new twists and turns about your story that you had no idea existed.

This is why our scene outline is just a guidepost. It's not set in stone because as you start writing, the story will take on a life of its own. You want to embrace it, but the downside is that doing so can sometimes screw up all the neat stuff you had planned. Maybe that big Act II turning point was supposed to take place on a space station, but that space station ended up being destroyed at the end of Act I. You'll have to figure that out.

Because everything is still shifting and moving, you need to go into your first draft understanding that things could change drastically by the time you are finished. The best way to combat this is to write what I love to call a "poop draft." I've also heard it called a "vomit draft," but I prefer "poop draft" because poop is funnier than vomit.

The idea behind a poop draft is that you fly through the thing. You get it done as quickly as possible, not worrying about typos or grammar or getting anything perfect. You just want to get your full story out of your head as fast as you can.

Many new screenwriters think the script has to be perfect from the start. That's not how it works. The script starts off kind of "meh," but you keep twisting and prodding and tweaking it until something turns out good. So it's OK if your first draft is bad. In fact, I can pretty much promise you that the first draft of your script will be bad. So you should embrace it! Why waste days writing and rewriting a scene to get it completely perfect when, after you finish your first draft, you might realize the scene really doesn't serve the purpose it was supposed to and you need to cut it?

By doing a poop draft, you are making things easier for yourself down the road. Plus, although many people don't realize it, rewriting is a boatload easier than writing. It's easier to rework a scene and punch it up than it is to come up with something from scratch. So you want to get this hard bit out of the way so you can get to the good stuff.

Make Time to Write

This is one of those things that is so obvious, but for some reason people struggle with it. A lot of people say, "I want to be a writer," but what they really mean is, "I want to have written." They want a finished product without having put in the work. I'm sorry, but it just doesn't work like that. If you want to be a writer, you have to write. Remember the name of this book? Finish the freakin' script and don't procrastinate.

It helps to write with a deadline in mind. I like to say, "I'll write at least four pages a day every day until my script is done." That means it would take me at most a month to get a 120-page screenplay finished. If you are a working parent and don't have that much time, that's OK. If you only write two pages a day — or even one page a day — that's OK too. The important thing is that you need to write something, and the faster you get the first draft done, the sooner you'll get to rewriting.

To help keep yourself motivated, there are several websites and word-counting apps for smartphones that count your pages for you, but personally, I'm a big fan of always keeping a piece of paper beside my desk. I record the date and then I write, and when I'm finished writing for the day, I mark down my page count. It's a simple, clear way for me to know that I'm moving forward, and nine times out of 10 I'm able to crank out a first draft within 10 to 14 days, depending on how busy my real-world responsibilities keep me.

What Works for You

Although in my class and in this book I advise doing a poop draft, you need to remember that I'm mostly dealing with novice writers. If you are someone who already knows your voice or your writing style, then do what already works for you. My main goal for this next section is just to get you to finish your first draft, no matter what approach you take.

Assignment Time

Plan your writing schedule. Know going into it when and how you will make time to write a screenplay.

Did you figure out an exact schedule? Did you warn your family members, loved ones and close friends that this is a priority for you, and that for the next 30 days or so you have to make time to write? If not, then do it! Get the word out there. Not only will they be more understanding when you can't spend time with them, but it also will help make you accountable, because now everyone you know and love will know about your screenplay.

CHAPTER FOURTEEN

Getting Through Act I

I love Act I. It's the easiest act to write in the whole screenplay. Everything you need to know is there in your pitch and character arc. All you are doing is looking at Act III and saying "OK, for XYZ to happen, then I need to start with ABC." That's it. Act I is all about the setup, introducing your characters and the world they live in, something shaking up that world and your character deciding to take a journey that will change them.

The biggest problem baby writers have with Act I is either they didn't plan right when doing their outlines or they forget that the first draft isn't a final draft. No one sits down and writes a perfect final draft of a screenplay in one sitting. It's just not how it's done. So no matter how hard your inner editor tries to break free and make you go back to rewrite parts of Act I, don't do it. You are way better off finishing the script and then going back to change and tweak stuff later.

Let's say, for example, that after writing your Act I turning point, you decide that a major supporting character needed to die in that turning point, and that this event would be the impetus that really moves your protagonist forward. You could go back and restructure all of Act I to properly set up that death, but you risk getting stuck in editing hell. You don't want that.

Instead, keep moving forward. Pretend you did write that scene with the death and that the scene was properly set up. Go into Act II as if it happened, and have your characters respond and act as if it happened. You can still go back and fix it, and you will, but you should wait until you've made it through the first draft.

Openings

Openings are important. If you don't have a good opening scene, no one will read the rest of your script. So what hooks a reader? Common ways may depend on your genre:

- Romantic comedy — show your protagonist getting dumped or otherwise hurt
- Comedy — show something crazy off-the-wall funny
- Action — show an explosion or big action sequence
- Horror — show someone getting killed
- Fantasy — show something epic

Please keep in mind that I'm not saying if you are doing X genre, your opening scene must be X. I'm simply saying that the opening scene often sets the tone of the movie.

Your main characters don't even have to be in the opening. Remember, the opening needs to set the tone of your movie. So go back to your pitch, see what your tone is and make sure that tone is clear in the opening.

The opening is a promise to your readers and viewers. It's saying, "Hey, this is the kind of story I'm going to tell." For example, if you are writing a serious adult drama and the opening is a massive car chase that ends in a huge explosion, and then you never have any more action in the rest of your screenplay, that's bad because the audience will be expecting more action and will be disappointed or confused when they never get it again.

"Virgin Dad" Rough Opening

So here is the unedited rough of my opening scene of "Virgin Dad." The first thing you should note is just how rough it is. I made sure that even when "Finish the Script" was edited, my amazing editor didn't fix the typos or mistakes here because I want you to see just how rough my first take of a scene is.

```
EXT. HAVEN SPERM BANK FOR THE GIFTED - DAY

LEGEND: 12 Years Ago

Description of whatever the bank looks
like.

INT. HAVEN SPERM BANK FOR THE GIFTED -
MOMENTS LATER

EUGENE BAKER stands at the front of a long
line of impatient nerdy men. He's lanky
with tight jeans blah blah descriptions.

Sitting behind the desk, like a bored bank
teller is a homely HAIRY MAN.
```

							EUGENE
					This is a bank isn't it? I want
					to withdrawal my deposit.

							HAIRY MAN
					You can't.

							EUGENE
					It's mine. I want it back!

							HAIRY MAN
					You signed the paperwork, buddy.
					Get lost.

							EUGENE
					You don't understand. I needed a
					brand new rubric cube for my
					experiment but low and behold I
					was able to disprove the weight
					of chicken without it.

Eugene slams his hand on the counter,
revealing a wad of cash.

							EUGENE
					I want my (funny word for sperm)
					back.

The Hairy Man grimaces and growls, but
Eugene still doesn't back down.

							EUGENE
					I will report you to the FCC.
					That's the Federal Trade
					Commission encase some of your
					inferior intellect couldn't
					tell.

The Hairy Man punches Eugene in the face,
knocking him out cold.

```
EXT. TIMEBOX SQUARED - DAY

LEGEND: Now.

Timebox is a research facility outside
of...
```

Before we get to the problems, there are a few things you should be aware of. The biggest is how I started the scene. We jumped right in at the sperm bank with Eugene mid-conversation with the hairy man. This is important because we want to hook our audience right away. If we had seen Eugene walking into the bank and up to the man, and listened to the first half of their conversation, it would've been boring. So instead we jumped right in where we needed to. Not only is this more interesting, but it also makes Eugene a more active character. He is doing something on-screen instead of merely reacting to something that is happening to him.

In addition to hooking the reader, this specific scene has two main points. First, it introduces us to Eugene. He's at a sperm bank trying to withdraw a deposit, which right away says a lot about his character. Then when the hairy man gets aggressive, Eugene has no clue. He doesn't see any of the warning signs that he's about to get punched in the face.

The other major thing we do in this scene is set up how Eugene could be a virgin and have a kid. That's done. Him being at the bank sets that up fine.

Scanning over the scene, though, there are a few problems. Obviously I need to go back and fill in description lines of things like "blah blah blah" or jokes. But more than that, I don't like the punch at the end. It just sort of happens, and if "Virgin Dad" were meant to be a studio comedy, then that kind of slapstick humor would be OK. In my case, it's the completely wrong tone for what I'm going for and it needs to be addressed.

So I have two options. I can just blow ahead and not worry about the scene until later, or I could rewrite it now. Guess what I'm going to do? I'm going to keep on going, and I'll address the opening scene again in my rewrite. Now that the rough version has been written and it's really bad, I have a feeling it needs to be set somewhere else and focus on something different. I could probably come up with a lot of nice ideas for how to change the scene now, but I'd rather not. I'd rather spend the first draft getting to know who Eugene is, and then once I have a clearer view of the whole story, I'll come back and whip something up.

Remember that pages 3 to 10 are all about exploring the world your protagonist lives in. It's all the setup for the character arc, seeing how your protagonist interacts with the world, and it needs to be engaging and interesting enough to win over your audience. This is the point when someone is going to decide whether to read your whole script or not, and nine times out of 10, interesting characters are the way to seal the deal.

Let's look at pages 3 to 10 from "Virgin Dad." After going through them once, I did go back and clean them up real quick, but for the most part the only editing done was fixing typos and things like that.

EXT. TIMEBOX SQUARED - TWILIGHT

Legend: Now

TimeBox Squared is a research facility in the farmland just north of Washington, D.C. The hills are rolling and the monstrosity of a building looks out of place in the twilight of the setting sun.

INT. EUGENE'S LAB - CONTINUOUS

A much older Eugene but still lanky and nerdy stands on the floor surrounded by thousands of ball bearings each no larger than his pinky nail.

The steel balls roll around the room as if spilled, but instead of slowing down and coming to rest they speed up and start forming a pattern as they systematically scour the room.

Holding his breath in excitement, Eugene glances at the tablet screen in his hands. There are flying numbers and stats.

Flashing in red the screen reds: TARGET NOT FOUND.

     EUGENE
    (cursing)
  Black-hole-sucking trapezoid!

The balls come to a halt.

The door opens and BART enters. He's chunky around the middle with an already bald head before he even hits 40.

     BART
  No luck?

                    EUGENE
          The numbers are right. There's
          no reason they shouldn't find
          the threat.

Bart picks up a soda can with a
radioactive symbol marked on it and tosses
it to Eugene.

                    EUGENE
          Careful with that. It's type 14
          plutonium. It could eradicate us
          within minutes.

                    BART
          It's Coke. It wouldn't even
          sterilize us. Not that it would
          matter to you.

                    EUGENE
          Children are a waste of time. My
          sister has a kid and her life is
          all about it. She could have had
          an amazing career as a cellist,
          but gave it all up for him.

                    BART
          The babies are a pain, but the
          babymak—

                    EUGENE
          The way I see it, if Nikola
          Tesla can be asexual there is no
          reason I can't.

                    BART
          You don't know what you're
          missing, if you know what I'm
          saying.

Bart spins his hands counterclockwise as
if he were spinning a record disc.

                    EUGENE
          I assure you that I quite, in
          fact, don't know.

Bart kicks one of the balls.

                    BART
          Then it's a good thing you don't
          have a family, 'cause Pearson is
          expecting you to have these
          fixed by morning, and you know—

Eugene freezes as if caught in headlights.

                    BART
          What?

                    EUGENE
          My sister is going to kill me.

EXT. CHLOEY'S HOUSE - NIGHT

Eugene parks a bicycle on the wraparound front porch of the Victorian house.

The yard is kept and there is a soccer-mom car in the driveway.

INT. CHLOEY'S KITCHEN - MOMENTS LATER

Eugene enters and gulps when he sees a single piece of birthday cake opposite Chloey. She's a healthy-looking girl — not fat, but definitely not an anorexic model. She has short blond hair and big blue eyes.

                    CHLOEY
          You promised.

                    EUGENE
          I know.

                    CHLOEY
          And what did you say?

                    EUGENE
          I said —

                    CHLOEY
          I was being rhetorical.

                    EUGENE
          I knew that.

Chloey takes the plate with the cake and
lifts it. Her wrist shakes with intention.

                    EUGENE
          No, don't!

                    CHLOEY
          You know the rules.

                    EUGENE
          But it's not right!

Chloey takes the cake and smashes it in
Eugene's face. He screams like a girl and
drops to the floor.

                    CHLOEY
          Next time you promise to be
          here, actually be here. Zax went
          to bed crying.

Eugene frantically tries to wipe off the
cake. It smears and he panics even more as
if it's dog poop.

                    EUGENE
          The punishment is by far
          outweighed. This is my Tuesday
          shirt and I don't do laundry
          again unti—

                    CHLOEY
          Do what you want with me. I'm
          your sister. I know you. My son
          is 6 and you made him cry. Don't
          do it again!

                    EUGENE
          I'm sorry.

Chloey points to the fridge.

                    CHLOEY
          There is another piece in there
          for you.

                    EUGENE
          With extra frosting?

                    CHLOEY
          Just the way you like it.

Eugene opens the fridge and looks inside.
Other than the cake wrapped to go, it's
pretty bare.

                    EUGENE
          You really should go grocery
          shopping.

                    CHLOEY
          I get paid Friday and we have
          enough in the freezer until
          then. Or do you want to critique
          my mom skills?

                    EUGENE
          No. No criticization there.

                    CHLOEY
          You'll come by this weekend?

                    EUGENE
          Yes. I have a big thing for work
          tomorrow but I'll come Saturday.

Chloey smiles.

Eugene dips into his coat pocket and pulls
several hundred dollar bills out of his
wallet. As Chloey escorts him to the front
door, he drops them onto the counter where
she's not looking.

EXT. DOWNTOWN BETHESDA - MOMENTS LATER

Eugene in helmet and flashing lights rides
his bike through downtown Bethesda. The
cake is strapped to a basket on his
handlebars.

EXT. EUGENE'S APARTMENT BUILDING LOBBY -
MOMENTS LATER

Eugene bolts his bike to a stand outside
of an apartment building.

INT. EUGENE'S APARTMENT - MOMENTS LATER

The apartment is big and spotless. It's
not fancy. Instead it's quite geek chic,
but to the point that the place doesn't
feel warm or lived in.

Eugene sits alone in his apartment eating
his cake.

So the first thing you notice is the structure. It's a few quick scenes and almost identical to my outline. We have:
- Eugene at work
- Eugene at Chloey's
- Eugene at home

In the first scene we set up the scientific world Eugene works in. We understand that some big deal is on the line and we are introduced to Bart. The hardest part of this scene is that science is boring on the screen. You don't want to see someone standing around doing math. You need to think visually. So the hardest part about writing this draft of the scene was trying to visually express Eugene's scientific endeavors. Ultimately he's creating a fancy targeting system that can properly asses threats. The ball bearings were a way to show it visually. In later drafts I may scrap it, but for now it's OK.

The scene with Chloey was fun because right away there was conflict. We've not talked about it yet, but every scene should have conflict. We will go over that when rewriting, but you'll notice that scenes that include heavy conflict are just more fun to write.

The biggest thing that happened with this scene is that even though I had wanted Chloey to be Eugene's cousin, it just didn't work out that way. There ended up being a lot of exposition, and so instead of spending time trying to explain the relationship, I just scrapped it. There were too many questions with her as his cousin. Why are they close? What happened to his parents? Where are her parents? It was easier to say "screw it" and make them brother and sister.

I also instantly liked Chloey's character. She's not what I had first planned, but I love how she stands up to Eugene and puts him in his place. There's also a sense of love between the two. Her having money trouble just sort of happened, and it's a good thing it did because it gives us a chance to see a different side of Eugene. We get to see him actually act empathetically, which isn't easy for him.

The final scene in this sequence is Eugene sitting home alone. It's done in a matter of seconds but it offers a nice, quiet moment and it really makes him feel alone with all his junk without being overly done. If I had him sighing or frowning, it would have been too much. Instead we just see him in his environment, and what makes it more sad is that he has no idea just how pathetic and lonely he really is.

So there are problems with these first pages, but we aren't worried about them yet. In later drafts I will completely rework these scenes, fix the horrible dialogue and gut anything that's indulgent or otherwise a waste of time. However, for now it does its job. We get to see Eugene exist in this little bubble, and next we will see that bubble popped and him struggling to keep control of his life.

Up until now you've been building your protagonist's world. You've hooked the reader in your opening and then you explored your hero's life and flaws over the course of the next five to 10 pages. Now it's time to shake things up.

You should be excited, because everything so far has been building up to this. This is the real start of your character's journey, the first phase of their changing life.

The biggest problem with the catalyst scene is that it can be very passive. Depending on what is shocking the protagonist out of their world, you may have to be really creative to keep your protagonist from just being along for the ride.

One good way to make the catalyst moment more active way is to have your protagonist initiate it. So let's say that the catalyst moment is your main character being fired from the police force. The actual act of firing will be done by the officer's superiors, but the reason for the firing could be something your protagonist did in Act I — even better if your protagonist's flaw is responsible for that action.

Of course, the catalyst can't always be a result of the protagonist's actions, but you can still put the control back in your protagonist's hands. Let's say you're writing a fantasy piece in which the catalyst is a dragon burning down the town and killing the protagonist's parents, launching your character on a revenge quest for the rest of the movie. Then during the attack, don't have the protagonist sitting on their butt or just running for their life. Have them actively trying to save people or something more proactive.

Let's look at the catalyst scene in "Virgin Dad."

```
INT. EUGENE'S APARTMENT - MORNING

The sun is shining bright on Eugene's
face. He's surrounded by the metal balls,
and a puddle of drool has formed on his
tablet.

Alarms sound like a spaceship under
attack.

Eugene bolts upright. He looks at his
Darth Vader watch and then jumps up and
throws his tablet and everything into his
bag.
```

INT. EUGENE'S APARTMENT BUILDING LOBBY - MOMENTS LATER

The stairwell opens and Eugene flies out of it, running into RAMIREZ, a well-to-do-looking lawyer in his 50s.

> EUGENE
> You should watch where you are going!

Eugene stands and moves toward the door.

Ramirez looks down at a paper and then up at Eugene.

> RAMIREZ
> Are you Eugene Baker?

> EUGENE
> No.

Eugene exits the building.

EXT. EUGENE'S APARTMENT BUILDING - MOMENTS LATER

Eugene exits in a hurry, followed by Ramirez.

> RAMIREZ
> You aren't Eugene Baker?

> EUGENE
> No, I'm Dr. Eugene Baker, ScD.

> RAMIREZ
> Oh, excellent. I wasn't sure if I was going to be able to track you down-

                    EUGENE
          If this is about my proof
          disproving the molecular theory
          of Carson's main principle,
          then-

                    RAMIREZ
          This is about your daughter.

Eugene pauses for a moment and then
laughs.

                    EUGENE
          I assure you I don't have a
          daughter.

Eugene and Ramirez walk past a town car.
META sits in the front seat. She watches
as the two pass and disappear around a
corner.

She gets out of the car and follows.

EXT. DOWNTOWN BETHESDA - MOMENTS LATER

Eugene continues power walking while
Ramirez looses his breath and lags behind.

Meta passes Ramirez. He tries to grab her
but misses.

Meta reaches Eugene and tugs on his shirt.

Eugene stops and looks at her.

                    EUGENE
          I am certain on some level this
          must have been an extremely
          well- thought-out prank, but my
          sense of humor isn't what you'd
          call-

                    META
          Please tell me you're not him.

Meta is looking at Ramirez.

                    META
          This can't be the guy. It's
          wrong.

Ramirez catches up, panting for breath.

                   RAMIREZ
This is him.

                    META
          No, no, no, no. Look at him!

Eugene stands as if offended.

                   EUGENE
          What is wrong with me?

                    META
          Well, for starters, you're a
          nerd and you clearly don't know
          how to dress yourself.

                   EUGENE
          Smart words coming from a thing
          with blue hair.

                    META
          My hair is part of my branding!

                   EUGENE
          If you do not desist following
          me, I will resort to calling the
          police.

Ramirez fumbles some paperwork.

                    RAMIREZ
          June 11th at the sperm bank in-

Eugene's' eyes go wide.

                    EUGENE
          What?

                    META
          My mom worked at the bank. She
          used your junk to make her self
          pregnant and then put you on the
          birth certificate.

                    EUGENE
          I'm your father?

                    META
          Supposedly.

                    EUGENE
          I don't have time for this. I'm
          on my way to an important
          meeting.

                    RAMIREZ
          I was XXXX's lawyer, and I
          assure you: You are her
          biological father and legal
          guardian.

                    EUGENE
          Call me next week and we will
          get this figured out.

                    RAMIREZ
          We don't have time. Either you
          take her in now, or I'll have to
          turn her over to child services,
          which is against XXX's wishes.

Eugene's phone rings and it's the Darth
Vader alarm. His phone reads "late!!!"

> EUGENE
> Fine, come with me.

> RAMIREZ
> Oh, excellent. XXX would've been so happy. If we can just find a place-

> EUGENE
> I really have to go. Either she comes with me or not.

> RAMIREZ
> It's up to you.

> META
> What about my stuff?

> EUGENE
> I'll buy you new stuff. We need to go now.

Meta turns to Ramirez.

> META
> I'll be fine.

> RAMIREZ
> I'll have the paperwork sent over, and we really need to schedule a time to go over it all.

> EUGENE
> Fine.

Eugene and Meta enter a subway entrance.

This whole catalyst sequence is bad. I mean really bad. It's *way* too long, the dialogue is way to expositional, the plot doesn't make sense and I'm not 100% sold on everyone's actions. But it's OK that it's bad. This is going to be one of the hardest scenes to write in the whole movie because it needs to do so much.

Part of my problem is that I still don't know my characters as well as I should. There's nothing I can really do about that except spend more time with them. So I just need to remind myself that by the time we finish the first draft, I'll have a much better understanding of who they are and then I can fix this horrendous scene.

One of the things I do like about the scene — and a good thing for you to keep in mind — is that it's not static. Scenes like this one can have so much exposition that they get severely bogged down and become boring. Eugene being late for a meeting and not wanting to bother with Ramirez and Meta gives the scene a sense of urgency that is physically expressed by them moving outside. Navigating the streets and curbs during their encounter gives me tons of stuff to play around with when I sit down and really work the scene over. Maybe Eugene gets honked at by a car or almost hit by someone. There's lots of stuff to do!

Off the top of my head, the biggest thing I'm questioning now is Ramirez's character. His only purpose is being an authority figure and spouting exposition. We know that Eugene loses Meta at the end of Act II, and Ramirez is meant to be the person who takes her away, the overseeing force.

Looking at it now, however, I'm thinking I really don't need him. At 12 years old, Meta is way too young to be on her own, but she's not stupid and it's not implausible that she took a taxi or was otherwise able to get to Eugene on her own. So by cutting Ramirez completely, I should be able to kill a lot of the dead weight in the scene and refocus it so that Meta and Eugene get all the attention. But I'm not going to worry about that at the moment. For now, I'm going to keep writing!

The rest of Act I should be really simple and fun to write. It's your protagonist dealing with the new world or situation that the catalyst threw them into.

The only thing to keep in mind is that, as always, you want to make sure your protagonist isn't being passive. In a superhero movie, this is the part of the story in which something happens that gives them their powers. In "Spider-Man" it's when Peter ends up at Oscorp and becomes Spider-Man; he then embraces his powers and learns to use them going into Act II.

Act I always involves your main character feeling uncomfortable with being thrown into new situations, and it's always fun. Just because it's new doesn't mean your protagonist has to be what often is called a "reluctant hero." Your protagonist can mostly embrace the new world but still to a certain extent be failing or somehow not dealing with it well. However, after you play around in the new situation for awhile, there will be a point at which your protagonist must officially and formally embrace it. That's the turning point we talked about.

So in "Virgin Dad," the rest of my Act I went a lot like my outline: Eugene traveled to work with Meta on the subway. He got to work and gave his presentation. It went badly. He did a paternity test. And then he went to Chloey's. The scene at Chloey's is my Act I turning point:

INT. CHLOEY'S LIVING ROOM - LATER

Chloey and Eugene stand in a doorway watching Meta. She's sitting at the dinning room table playing a board game with Zax.

> CHLOEY
> She has grandma's eyes.

> EGUENE
> Will you take her?

> CHLOEY
> Excuse me?

Eugene pulls out a checkbook.

> EUGENE
> If money is an issue, I am more than willing to cover the cost of her living expenses and bills.

> CHLOEY
> I know you are my older brother and a lot smarter than I am, but open your eyes and look at her.

Chloey points through the doorway at Meta.

> CHLOEY
> She is your daughter. She is half you, and she has no family. Do you remember what that was like? Do you remember when Mom and Dad died and how it was moving from home to home? Do you want that for her?

Eugene looks at Meta. She's playing a

board game with Zax and laughing.

                    EGUENE
          I wouldn't want that for anyone.
          Especially her.

                    CHLOEY
          It's not just you anymore that
          you have to worry about. You
          need to step up and be a father.

                    EUGENE
          I'm not really the father type.

                    CHLOEY
          Anyone who has ever met you
          knows that, but you should've
          thought of that before you
          locked your sperm in a bank and
          then had it illegally used to
          produce a kid.

Eugene looks ruffled.

                    EUGENE
          Now wait just a darn second! I
          took careful evaluation of my
          actions and since at the time I
          was already passing my prime, it
          made sense to store my sperm. I
          had no way of being able to
          predict that-

Chloey is laughing.

                    CHLOEY
          I know, and to be honest, this
          may be the best thing ever to
          happened to you.

                    EUGENE
          Well, I guess if Anakin
          Skywalker can do it, so can I.

So let's do this. Where do I start?

          CHLOEY
Start with the basics, like feeding her, making sure she's clean and has a place to sleep.

          EUGENE
Ohhh, so like Sparky, when we were kids?

          CHLOEY
Meta will be slightly more complicated than taking care of a puppy. Though I would put down newspaper in case she decides to mark her territory.

          EUGENE
I had seen that mentioned in a documentary about a South-African tribe, but I thought the whole thing was-

Chloey is laughing again.

          EUGENE
You were being sarcastic again, weren't you?

Chloey smiles and kisses her brother on the cheek.

The thing to remember is that the turning point must involve your protagonist fully accepting the journey that their character arc is all about. In this case, "Virgin Dad" is all about Eugene realizing the importance of family and him becoming a father. His flaw is that he thinks his work in science is more important than family. So for him to change, he has to embrace his new situation, and that's why the most important part of the previous scene is Eugene saying he's going to keep Meta. It's also why the scene ends almost right after that. There's no point in lingering. Act I is over. We got what we wanted and it's time to move on.

Assignment Time

Write Act I of your screenplay!

CHAPTER FIFTEEN

Getting Through Act II

Act II is a nightmare. It's the hardest freakin' thing to write in the whole screenplay. Act I is all about setting up the characters and their world. Act III is about wrapping up all the loose ends. This means that Act II is a playground in which there are no rules. Look back at my beat sheet for "Virgin Dad." There are hardly any beats in Act II because it's a free range. It's where you as the screenwriter really get to define your story and your voice.

It's best to think of Act II in two parts. Part 1 is from pages 30 to 60, and Part 2 is from pages 60 to 90.

If you remember our character arcs, everything is lost at the end of Act II. It's when our protagonist hits rock bottom. But before they can get there, we need to build them up first, and that's really the purpose of the entire first half of Act II — making everything better so that when we destroy it, our protagonist will hurt even more.

In a romantic comedy, this is the honeymoon phase. It's where the couple really start to fall in love and connect with each other. In a superhero movie, this is where the hero learns their powers. In an adventure story, it's the light action fluff that goes super well.

Thematically speaking, remember that our protagonist left Act I on a mission. They recognized a flaw and they started on a journey of growth and change. So this first bit of the journey is them embracing their new life, and it's going pretty well for them.

This doesn't mean that pages 30 to 60 are conflict-free or boring. It just means that this is normally when the protagonist is the most happy and for a time thinks, "Hey, I can change and fix this flaw of mine." Failure is even more painful when things are going well, so that's why it's important that this part of your character's journey is lighter than what's coming.

If you are struggling with what needs to happen in this long stretch, think specifically about what you will destroy later in the movie. There are three main areas of a character's life: their work life, their home life and their love life. When we hurt them at the end of Act II, we normally do everything we can to wound them on all fronts. We do our best to take everything away from them and crush them. If the plan for that is them losing these things, the first part of Act II needs to make these things better and stronger.

In many cases, this is what a lot of writers refer to as the "B" story. If the main movie plot is your "A" story, the "B" story is where you really ramp up the subplots. In a big action movie, this may be the point where a love interest and their storyline is introduced.

I won't bore you with 30 pages of script, but Act II of "Virgin Dad" focuses on three things: Eugene's new fatherhood, his accomplishments at work and the rest of his home and family life. As Eugene is learning to be a father, it doesn't always work out well — in fact, it often ends badly in a humorous way — but on the whole he's trying, and he and Meta are growing closer. We also expanded the cast and set up the science fair that will be a major location in Act III as well as become a big plot point at the end of Act II.

At work Eugene is doing great. He's really started to figure out his project and fix the problem he was up against; now he just needs to finish it so he can properly present it and earn the $20 million for his company.

With regard to his home life, Eugene has been spending more time with Chloey and Zax. For the first time since Eugene was a boy, he has a family unit. Also I scrapped the character of Johanna, who I thought was going to be Meta's science teacher, and instead made Chloey a guidance counselor at Meta's school. It just makes more sense for her to serve that role so we can get to know her better instead of wasting time with a bit character.

Why do I spend time on these three things? Because at the end of Act II, Eugene will lose Meta, he will get fired from his job and he will have made Chloey so furious that she refuses to even speak to him.

Whereas the first half of Act II is all about building up a character and their world, the midpoint is the turning point. It's when things start to go bad. In many ways it foreshadows the end of Act II.

The important thing to remember about the midpoint is your character's arc. In Act I they either chose or were somehow forced to fix their flaw. They spent the first half of Act of II living in a happier world as they actively tried to be a better person. Somewhere at or near the midpoint, they should recommit to that journey.

As an example, I'm going to share the midpoint scene from Act II of "Virgin Dad." The bonding between Meta and Eugene has been hit or miss, but they have been slowly growing closer. In the scene directly before this one, Eugene embarrasses Meta in front of a boy, and at the end of that scene we discover Meta has had a period and it has seeped through her white shorts, furthering her embarrassment.

INT. SCHOOL HALLWAY - MOMENTS LATER

Eugene raps on the door to the girl's bathroom.

          EUGENE
  Meta?

There is no response. After a pause, Eugene enters.

INT. GIRL'S BATHROOM - CONTINUOUS

Eugene enters and doesn't see Meta. Leaning over, he spots her feet behind one of the closed stall doors.

          EUGENE
  Are you all right?

          META
  Oh my god, will you shut up and
  go away?

          EUGENE
  I'm not going without you. What
  can I do to help?

          META
  Nothing! I don't want you. I
  want Mom.

          EUGENE
  I know it hurts, but I'm the one

who is here.

                    META
Get Chloey!

                    EUGENE
She already left to pick up Zax
from preschool.

                    META
Then get me anyone that isn't
you!

                    EUGENE
I know this is hard, but the
changes you are going through
are natural. You don't need to
be scared or-

                    META
I'm not scared. I know what a
period is.

                    EUGENE
Then put in a tampon or use a
pad and we'll go home, OK?

                    META
I can't.

                    EUGENE
Why not?

                    META
I don't have one. This is my
first period.

Eugene nods and then leaves the bathroom.

                    META
Dad?

INT. SCHOOL HALLWAY - MOMENTS LATER

Eugene has walked down the hall and is in the process of ripping an emergency first-aid kit off the wall.

INT. GIRL'S BATHROOM - MOMENTS LATER

Eugene re-enters carrying the kit. He sets it down on the sink counter and then taps on Meta's stall.

> EUGENE
> I need your underwear.

> META
> Ewww, no.

> EUGENE
> Do you want me to help or not?

Meta sticks her dirty underwear out from under the stall. Eugene takes them.

> EUGENE
> First things first, I'm going to do my best to clean them.

Using soap and hot water, Eugene manages to get most of the blood out of the underwear. He then uses a wall hand dryer to dry them.

> EUGENE
> Lucky for us you are still in an early spotting stage. If this were a full-on period, I don't think this would work.

Taking gauze from the kit, Eugene wraps the gauze in toilet paper and then tapes the makeshift pad into the underwear.

Eugene passes the underwear back under the stall.

>   EUGENE
> How does that fit? Can you walk without it shifting?

>   META
> I think so. But what about my shorts?

>   EUGENE
> Hand them over.

She does and after rinsing them with hot water, Eugene removes peroxide from the kit and dabs it on the stain.

>   EUGENE
> Peroxide is perfect for removing stains from a porous surface like concrete, but with your shorts it won't do a perfect job because the fabric will have already absorbed some of the iron from your blood. Once we get home I can remove the stain completely, but for now this should be fine.

Eugene dries the shorts and then passes them back to Meta. A moment later she exits the stall and the stain is barely visible.

>   META
> Thank you.

>   EUGENE
> I'm glad I could help. On the way home, we will stop at a store and buy you some feminine products. I don't know the

>   merits of using a pad or a
>   tampon, but we can always call
>   Chloey and ask her.
>
>   META
>   Why does this stuff not sketch
>   you out like it normally does
>   with guys?
>
>   EUGENE
>   Why would it? It's basic
>   biology. And although biology is
>   not the most respected science,
>   it is still science — which
>   reminds me, we still need to
>   have The Talk tonight.
>
>   META
>   No, we really don't.
>
>   EUGENE
>   Yes we-
>
>   META
>   Dad, Logan is gay.
>
>   EUGENE
>   Well that's a comfort. In that
>   case, why don't we save The Talk
>   for another night?
>
> She smiles.

So by the end of the midpoint scene, Eugene and Meta are finally becoming a real family unit. Eugene has embraced the role of being a loving and caring father, while Meta has officially started to see him as an authority figure. Also, by going through this experience, they have already become a lot closer. This is great because in the next 20 to 30 pages, when we destroy their relationship, it will hurt that much more!

The midpoint of Act II is in many ways the moment of glory for your protagonist. Things have been going fairly well and everyone is happy. If we ended "Virgin Dad" now, it would be easy to assume that Eugene and Meta lived happily ever after. We aren't ending it now, though, because Eugene still hasn't finished his journey in becoming a better person. We want Eugene to realize that family is important and should come before his career. That hasn't happened yet. He's not yet been put in a situation in which he has to choose between the two. That situation will become our Act II turning point, and it will lead to his fall. But before he can fall, we have to build him up, and that's what the first half of Act II and the midpoint should be about — building the emotional world that you are going to destroy.

Now as for the scene we just read, as always, it has problems. The dialogue is too on the nose. There is too much talking and not enough action. It's also way too long, but you know what I'm going to tell you, right? I don't care. This is the first draft and we will deal with it later. For now my only goal is to finish the script.

The second half of Act II isn't as hard as the first half. In fact, it's one of my favorite parts to write. Why? Because there is one big question you should be asking: "How can I hurt my protagonist more?"

That's it. The second half of Act II is all about breaking down and destroying your protagonist, and if you did your job in the first half of Act II, most of what you need to do is already done for you.

In a romantic comedy, this would be the couple breaking up. In a superhero movie, it's the bad guy defeating the hero and about to invoke their master plan. In a fantasy epic, it's when the hero gets the big magic prize and it doesn't work.

So how do you destroy your protagonist? You do what we talked about before. Remember those things you were building up — the protagonist's love life, home life and career? Now you pull them out from under them. The only real secret is that the house of cards has to fall because of something your protagonist did. Most of the time this is a bad choice they made that's related to their flaw.

In "Virgin Dad," there is a good 20 pages in which Meta is building a board game for a competition. (It used to be a science fair, but somehow in the first half of Act II, I decided a board game convention with a contest was more unique and fun.) While she is doing that, everything at Eugene's work is starting to come undone. Because of bad time management since his new fatherhood, he's not finished his big AI project. After a series of all-nighters, he finally gets it done on the morning before it's due.

```
INT. EUGENE'S ROOM - MORNING

Eugene is asleep at his desk. Wires are
strewn everywhere, forming a massive nest,
and at its center are the newly finished
orbs. They are popped open so that the
wires can connect directly to their
processors.

Meta enters carrying a cup of orange juice
and a plate of runny eggs and bacon.
```

                    META
          Dad.

Eugene bolts upright, startled awake, and
his elbow whacks the cup of orange juice.
The cup flips and lands on the desk,
filling all of the open little orbs with
the sticky liquid.

                    EUGENE
          NO!

The orbs sizzle and little puffs of smoke
form over them.

                    EUGENE
          I have the biggest meeting in my
          life in a matter of hours. This
          can't be happening.

                    META
          I can fix them. I can clean
          them.

Eugene grabs her arm and points her toward
the door.

                    EUGENE
          Get out!

                    META
          But I can clean it up.

                    EUGENE
          You can't. So get your things
          and go to school. I'll see you
          tonight.

Upset, Meta turns away and leaves the
room.

INT. EUGENE'S APARTMENT - MOMENT'S LATER

Meta has on her backpack and slams the front door of the apartment as she leaves.

Eugene looks up toward the door. In doing so he see's Meta's game, Butterfly Storm, on the coffee table.

INT. EUGENE'S ROOM - MOMENT'S LATER

Eugene's messy desk has been cleared away and on it is Meta's game.

In Eugene's hand is one of the butterfly pieces. It's upside down, and we can see that the components are identical to those he used for the robot orbs.

Fiddling with it, he breaks the wings off the butterfly.

INT. EUGENE'S ROOM - LATER

It's a massacre. Each of the butterflies have been stripped for parts. Their wings and empty shells are strewn across the table.

The turning point for "Virgin Dad" is actually pretty simple and sweet. Eugene decides to destroy Meta's game so that he can use the parts to fix his work project. In the grand scheme it doesn't feel like that big of deal: he destroyed a little project so that his work can make

$20 million.

However, what you didn't see in that scene is all the emotional investment Meta put into that game. Destroying Butterfly Storm is such a big deal that it will completely wreck the relationship the two have been building since the end of Act I.

As for executing the turning point, it's pretty straightforward: the aftermath of Eugene's choice will run for pages upon pages. Rereading the turning point leaves me with only one really big problem: I *hate* how the orbs are ruined. It's cliche and stupid and poor writing. I need to sit down and really think about the best way to write that scene so that the orbs are ruined in a non-cheeseball way. But guess what? I'll worry about that later.

Assignment Time

Write Act II.

CHAPTER SIXTEEN

Getting Through Act III

If you've made it through Act II, then Act III is a breeze. All we are going to do now is wrap up the bits of plot points you already have.

Honestly, if you are going to skimp anywhere on the first draft of your screenplay, this is the place to do it. Why? Because depending on character arcs and things like that, your Act III may be extensively rewritten once you know your characters better.

So when writing Act III, stick as close to your outline as you want to. By this point your original plans may have already drastically changed. For example, in "Virgin Dad," the whole climax was supposed to take place at a science fair. So none of what I had planned works because now the big climax is at a GameCon convention.

However, even though my location and circumstances have changed, Eugene's character arc hasn't. He's still going through the same journey that I had originally planned. I just need to adapt it to fit into the new situation.

So going into Act III, I've taken everything away from Eugene. He was fired from his job, Meta has moved out and into Chloey's house, and Chloey refuses to see or speak to Eugene. Everything that Eugene cared about is gone.

The next thing I'm going to do, after letting him suffer for a bit, is make him realize his mistake. He knows he shouldn't have destroyed Meta's game, but he needs to really connect and understand that in doing so, he was being selfish and putting himself and his career before his daughter. This is what I referred to on the beat sheet as the epiphany moment.

In this case, I have Eugene sitting at home alone, staring into his empty apartment, when he starts hearing a beeping sound. All you need to know going into this scene is that throughout "Virgin Dad," Meta has been recording video blogs on YouTube. She's also really into gaming and that whole scene, but we never know why. I think when Eugene hits rock bottom, it would be really cool to have a scene in which he is skimming through Meta's videos, which would end up looking something like this:

```
INT. META'S ROOM - CONTINUOUS

Eugene hears the "beep" again and enters
the room. Meta's computer is on and there
is a flashing "new message" alert. It
beeps again and the counter jumps from 16
to 18.

Eugene touches the screen and sees that
the alert is for a new comment on YouTube.
He clicks through the link and a video of
Meta appears. It was uploaded less than
five minutes ago.
```

In the video, Meta is sitting in the back of a cab and crying.

                    META
          Hey, guys, it's GameTime! So
          remember Butterfly Storm, which
          I was so excited about demoing
          at GameCon? Well, that's not
          happening now. Why? You can
          thank my dad.

Meta pauses to catch her breath. She wipes the tears from her eyes, but she looks more angry than hurt.

                    META
          When Mom died I thought my life
          was over. I thought this was it
          and I'm alone for now and
          forever. Then I found out I had
          a dad and thought, sure, things
          wouldn't be the same, but at
          least I'd have a family and a
          place to call home. Turns out I
          was being naive.

The cab takes an abrupt turn and Meta looks out the window.

                    META
          OK, I gotta go. I'll update you
          on the new Butterfly Storm
          prototype once I have time to
          actually build it. I just wanted
          to give you all a heads up that
          it won't be at the show
          tomorrow.

The video ends and a screen pops up showing old videos of Meta. In each she has different-colored hair.

Eugene scrolls through and finds Meta's

first video. It's less than five months old. He plays it.

Meta appears on-screen again. This time her standard blue hair is gone and she's now sporting a bleached white mop with green tips.

> META
> Hey, guys. I'm Meta, and it's GameTime. This is my vlog of games and all things games related. For this first video I thought it would be cool to talk about my all-time favorite game and how I got into gaming.

INT. HOSPITAL ROOM - NIGHT

Meta sits on the foot of a hospital bed. She's younger now and has hot pink hair. Lying in the bed is VIVIAN, Meta's mom.

> META
> So what do we have tonight, more Monopoly or checkers?

> VIVIAN
> I know you hate that stuff.

> META
> Who doesn't? It's boring.

> VIVIAN
> Which is why I bribed a nurse and got something cool.

Vivian lifts up a pillow on the bed beside her to reveal Pandemic, the board game.

                    VIVIAN
          It's a co-op game, which means
          we work together to try and save
          the planet from a pandemic that
          could kill all human life.

Meta squints as if interested but not
wanting to admit it.

                    META
          OK, maybe we can try that one.

INT. HOSPITAL ROOM - DAY

Meta and Vivian sit playing Compounded, a
science-based board game that has the
periodic table as a score track.

                    META (V.O.)
          After Pandemic, I was hooked. I
          didn't know the depth of indie
          games or how much better they
          were than anything lame put out
          by Hasbro.

Meta and Vivian laugh as they flip a tile
and reveal a lab fire, which destroys most
of the board.

                    META (V.O.)
          These past few months have been
          the hardest of my life, but
          through gaming they also have
          also become some of the best
          memories I will ever have of my
          mother.

INT. META'S ROOM - NIGHT

Eugene is still watching the video of
Meta.

                    META
          So that's what I want to do with
          this vlog. I want to share my
          love of games with you!

The very second the video ends, Eugene
reaches forward and opens the next.

INT. META'S ROOM - SUNRISE

The golden rays of the sun flood through
the windows and onto Eugene, who is still
watching YouTube videos of Meta. He has
managed to get caught up to the second
newest one. In it, Meta is showing off
Butterfly Storm.

                    META
          I'm super-cereal about this con,
          and I think Butterfly Storm has
          a chance to win. So if you guys
          come out for it, make sure you
          find me so you can demo the
          game!

Eugene sighs and leans back in his chair.

                    EUGENE
          Oh, Meta.

For an epiphany moment, it's a tad over the top, but that's fine. This is the first draft and I can work it over later. What's important is that Eugene realizes just how big of a deal the board game was to Meta. Now he gets it. He knows that he should've chosen her over his work instead of the other way around.

Having learned from his mistake, now Eugene needs to make

amends, and to be honest I struggled with how to do that. Other than his orbs, so far Eugene hasn't had any physical property that is special to him. And he lost the orbs when he was fired because they were company property.

To fix this, I have a cool idea. After watching Meta's videos, he sees an old trophy on his mantel. It will be steampunkish and covered with moving gears and parts. I can set it up so that it's something he won as a kid at a science fair, and it will be his most prized possession. That way when Eugene goes to make amends, he can destroy the trophy and use its pieces to fix Meta's game. Once that's completed, the story will move to the convention center in D.C., and the whole climax will be set at GameCon.

Keep in mind, though, that the real ending isn't the big climax in which the good guy takes on the bad guy. The real end of the movie is that final temptation that happens during the climax. It's that moment in which the protagonist is presented with a choice, and they must either choose for good this new path of enlightenment or fall back on their old ways.

In the case of Eugene, I'm going to have a government guy from the DoD offer him a prestigious job. It will require relocating and crazy hours, but it will pay well. But because the job wouldn't be a good one for him to have while being a single father, he's going to turn it down. He will choose family over work, thus proving he has changed.

The end of a screenplay often is, in many ways, the poetic opposite of the beginning. So if you are stuck, go back and look at who your protagonist was in pages 3 to 10. If your character is exactly the same and you aren't doing an antihero-type story, then something is wrong.

A great example of this is in the movie "Up." During the whole movie, Carl has been trying to protect and save his house. It represents him holding on to his marriage and his memories of his dead wife. But when we get to the climax of the movie, Carl must sacrifice his house and his possessions so that he can save Russell. So by destroying the thing he loves most, he shows the audience that he has grown and is finally able to let go of the past.

Once you finish your big climax, in which your protagonist either completes or fails to complete their journey, your story is done. There is no reason to linger. Generally speaking, the final scene is just an epilogue that wraps up the the story and thematically ties everything together. The epilogue is the last scene that people will take home with them. So that ending really needs to evoke the emotion you want.

A movie doesn't have to have a happy ending. It just has to be satisfying for what you've been building up to. You can even kill your protagonist if you want, as long as the ending is still satisfying.

Right now I'm not sure how I want "Virgin Dad" to end. The final scene is normally something I don't even touch until I'm about halfway through the rewriting process. Because it needs to be thematic and work so well, it's often hard to write until more of your story is set in stone. So if for some reason you don't know how you want to end your movie, that's OK. This is the one scene I'll allow you to skip for now and write during the rewrite process.

Assignment Time
   Finish your first draft!

CHAPTER SEVENTEEN

Congratulations, you did it! You've finished your first draft and you are one step closer to having a finished screenplay!

The first thing you need to do is be very proud of yourself. You've worked your butt off and you almost have something to show for it.

You've now reached a major stepping point in the writing process. Your first draft is done. You should feel very, *very*, **very** proud about it. If you don't, then go back and think of where you were when we started this whole process. I've seen you grow as a writer. You should be proud.

But unfortunately, writing a first draft is just part of the battle. Writing is rewriting. It's the rewriting process that really helps writers stand out, because it's then that we make our work shine. It's also a grueling pain in the butt. There is a well-known phrase that refers to rewriting as "killing your baby." Yes, it sounds gruesome, but as a writer, your work in many ways is your baby. To make it the best it can be, you need to be willing to cut out anything that doesn't serve the whole story, even if it's small stuff you really like. So going into this, just keep in mind that you may need to kill your baby.

So remember *way* back when when we first started writing? Most of what we are about to do is repeating what you've already done. The big difference here is that you now know your characters and their world way more than you did before.

The biggest problem with most rewrites is that you start at Page 1, which is already probably the best-written page in the script. You tweak as you go, page after page, moving commas and enjoying your cleverness — all the while forgetting why you're rewriting the script.

Instead, stop thinking of words and pages and focus on goals. Are you trying to increase the rivalry between Helen and Chip? Then look through the script — actual printed script, not the one on-screen — and find the scenes with Helen and Chip. Figure out what could be changed in those scenes to meet your objectives. Then look for other scenes that help support the idea. Scribble on the paper. Scratch out lines. Write new ones. Then move on to your next goal. And your next one.

Concept Pass

The first thing you want to do at the rewrite stage is called the concept pass, which helps you assess how true you stayed to your original intention throughout the draft-writing process. Bust out your pitch and look at it. Your grasp of the story and characters has changed drastically since you first wrote the pitch, so read it over and see how it compares with what you wrote in your first draft.

This is where it gets tricky, because 95% of the time what you wrote did change. But that's actually OK. That's normal. More accurately, the question is whether what you wrote stayed true to the *spirit* of your original pitch. That's what we really need to worry about. Is what you have written spiritually close to what you originally set out to write? If it's not, then you need to ask why. What changed and was it for the better or worse? After this tutorial, I think you're probably pretty close to what you originally intended to write. If you disagree, let me know and we'll deal with it together.

Story Pass

This is the part where you just fill in plot holes. There should be tons — not because you are a bad planner, but because things changed as you wrote. You discovered new things, or you set up things in Act I and never used them again. So now is the time when you go back and get rid of all that junk.

For example, doing my story pass for "Virgin Dad," the very first scene I want to address is the opening. The original one at the sperm bank was just horrendous, and now that I now what my big story is, I want to go back and deal with it.

The biggest change in "Virgin Dad" was that we scrapped the science fair as the finale for a game convention. On top of that, Eugene destroys the prized trophy he won as a kid to fix Meta's game that he broke, so now I think the opening should be him winning that prize. That whole sequence would look something like this:

```
EXT. WASHINGTON CONVENTION CENTER - DAY

Legend: Then.

A 12-year-old EUGENE BAKER enters the
faded convention center. A stitched banner
```

hanging over the door reads, "Welcome to the National Science Fair."

As Eugene walks, a swishing sound is heard from the sides of his plaid corduroys, which are pulled way too high but still look better than his short-sleeve button-up shirt and red bow tie.

Trailing behind Eugene is a two-foot robot that looks like the bastard child of R2D2 and Wall-E. Its white body resembles an upside-down trash can while its head looks like a pair of modified night-vision googles.

INT. WASHINGTON CONVENTION CENTER - MOMENTS LATER

Eugene and his robot enter the main hall. Not a single woman or girl has straight hair and every boy is sporting some version of plaid. It's clearly the '80s.

INT. WASHINGTON CONVENTION CENTER SIDE HALL - MOMENTS LATER

Eugene follows his robot down a narrow side hall and stops abruptly when a pack of nerds appears from a crossway.

There are four nerds. One is fat, one is skinny, one is pimpled and JAKE, the leader of the bunch, is also the shortest and sports the thickest glasses.

                    JAKE
     You lost, Eugene? Maybe we can
     help you to the main hall.

The boys surround Eugene and his robot like a pack of hungry wolves.

                    EUGENE
          I know precisely where the main
          hall is and your intimidation
          tactics will not work on me.

                    JAKE
          Is that so?

Jake nods his head and the fat boy pins Eugene to the floor, flattening him so that he can't turn his head to look away.

Pimples and Skinny pick up Eugene's robot, each holding onto a side of it.

                    JAKE
          No cries for help?

                    EUGENE
          Nothing you can do can stop me
          from winning today. I've already
          outsmarted you.

Jake nods again and the other two boys smash the robot to the ground. The lenses on the robot's night vision googles shatter.

                    JAKE
          You sure you don't want to cry
          for your mommy?

                    EGUENE
          My mother is dead, which you are
          well aware of. And no matter
          what I say to you, we both know
          that you are going to destroy my
          robot no matter what.

                    JAKE
          That sounds about right, so why
          don't we get to the finale?

Jake and the other two boys take turns
kicking and stomping on the robot. It's
brutal. When they are done, all the bits
and pieces of it are broken off. The only
thing that remains is the solid metal
upside-down trash can that formed its
torso.

                    JAKE
          Good luck next year.

Fatso climbs off Eugene and the nerd-pack
recedes into a shadowy hallway.

Without saying a word, Jake picks up the
solid torso piece of his robot.

INT. NATIONAL SCIENCE FAIR SHOW FLOOR -
LATER

Eugene stands at a bare table with the
torso of his robot on it while three older
judges with clipboards look at him,
confused.

                    WOMAN JUDGE
          What exactly is it?

                    EUGENE
          It's a decoy, ma'am.

Eugene reaches out and applies pressure,
then twists the top of the torso. A door
opens to reveal a Rubik's-cube-sized
object covered in gears and cogs.

                    EGUENE
          I call it Topo.

>   WOMAN JUDGE
>   What does it do?
>
> Eugene points to the woman's clipboard.
>
>   EUGENE
>   May I?
>
> She hands Eugene a blank piece of paper
> and he sets Topo down on it. Topo spins to
> life. The gears swirl and it extends a pen
> and three wheels out of its bottom.
>
> Sketching as it goes, Topo dances across
> the paper, marking a topographic map of
> the entire convention center.
>
>
> INT. SCIENCE FAIR AWARD SHOW - LATER
>
> The judge stands onstage with Eugene
> beside her. She's handing him a trophy in
> the shape of an atom with spinning
> electrons.
>
> In the background with a No. 2 medal sits
> Jake with his arms crossed.

The new opening flowed really well when I was writing it. For example, now that I know who Eugene is, it was much easier to write his dialogue, even for a child version of him. It's also amazing how much better this scene is compared with my original opening scene.

Remember, the opening is supposed to set the tone of the movie. Because we are meeting Eugene for the first time, I really wanted to make it clear who he is as a character, and I think this scene is so much stronger than him being awkward at a sperm bank. For example, we see right off the bat that he's smart, only this time we don't learn it because he's using big words. Instead we learn it through the actions he takes. He not only created this cool robot, but he also managed to outsmart the nerd bullies.

The nerd bullies were unexpected and fun to write. I think it might be nice to make one of them Bart from Eugene's work. That way the opening scene ties in better. My gut instinct is to make Bart the fat kid and during the opening scene have him whisper, "Sorry." I think it will help make Bart more likable later.

You guys didn't read it, but the first draft of "Virgin Dad" ended with Meta losing the GameCon competition. I'm still going to keep that because now I really enjoy the symmetry of opening with Eugene winning and ending with her losing. Plus both events clearly define my two main characters.

Of course the new opening isn't perfect and needs work. For example, I want the destruction of the robot to be more violent, and that way when I rewrite the scene in which Eugene destroys Meta's game, I want to mimic some of the movements and descriptions so that my audience will be reminded of the earlier event.

But on whole it's a big step up from where we were before, and looking at it only from the perspective of a story pass, it does already help fill in some of the plot holes I created when writing my first draft.

Structure Pass

The next thing we need to look at is your overall structure. The idea is to approach the story in chunks, just like we did with your sequence and scene outline. I suggest making a list of your scenes, then writing down next to each what its point is. Remember, each scene *must* move the plot forward or develop character. If you can do both in a single scene, that's even better. If a scene does neither, then you need to either rewrite it so that it does or cut it altogether.

I'm a structure fiend, so "Virgin Dad" is pretty solid with its structure. Any changes I'll make will be because of changing characters or plot points, so I don't have any big examples to show you.

Character Pass

Your hero has changed since their conception. As a result, their character arc might also have changed, so the next thing we want to look at is your protagonist. How is their arc? How is their personality? What's working and what isn't working? You really need to dig down and take a hard look at your protagonist.

This step really needs to be all you. I can't tell you what to do here. You just need to look honestly at Eddie and figure out how you feel about him. Do you like him? Do you think he's acting like a normal person? Do you think he has an individual voice? What do you think is missing? What do you think is not working? What don't you like about him? Really take some time to scrutinize Eddie, and send me your thoughts and feelings about him. If you identify problems or things you don't like, then we can work together on how to fix them.

One of my screenwriting professors in college told me that as your protagonist moves through your story, they need to burn down their house and all bridges they cross so they can never go home again. It's very poetic sounding, but it makes sense. You want your protagonist to be active, and it's much easier to be active when there isn't an easy way out. So other than checking your character's journey, also evaluate how passive they are being throughout the story.

Of course part of your rewrite is making sure all your character arcs are right. You want to sit down and map out each character, not just your protagonist. Chloey is one of the better supporting characters in "Virgin Dad," so let's do a breakdown of her scenes.

- Night scene with cake
- Chloey learns that Meta is Eugene's daughter
- How-to-be-a-parent scene
- Advice scene two
- Scene with Meta after the midpoint
- Act II turning point, Part 2
- Act III — making amends
- Epilogue

For being such a major supporting character, she really isn't in the script that much — just eight scenes altogether. That means each of her scenes is even more important, because we have to maximize our time with her.

Right now she is only a supporting character. She exists to be the voice of reason that whispers in Eugene's ear, and later she is the support figure who is there for Meta when Eugene fails her. It's great that Chloey is supporting our leads, but it's not enough. As I mentioned when we first started talking about the supporting cast, each member must believe they are the stars of the story. In their heads, they are the lead actors in their own movie. Right now Chloey has nothing going on in her life. She has no big desires other than to be a good mother, sister and aunt — not that those are bad things, but for this story, they aren't enough.

To fix this, I'm going to introduce her husband. Before I wrote the first draft, I kind of assumed her husband was dead or left her. But somewhere when I was writing, Meta asked Chloey where Zax's dad was, and Chloey tells her that he's overseas. That idea has been sitting with me, and I think it would be cool if her husband were a military man. That way Chloey's story is more about her struggling to be the mom/sister/aunt at home who is keeping everything together while her husband is risking his life. It will be interesting to see her deal with the stress and the loneliness.

Plus at the end of Act II, it would be pretty epic if her husband went missing. And having the cool sci-fi AI and the Department of Defense in the story already is a nice way to intertwine Chloey's story with Eugene's. It would set us up so that in Act III, the technology Eugene has been building throughout the movie is then used to find Chloey's husband.

So I want to make a lot of changes, but not as many as you'd expect. I might need to add one or two scenes to make these changes, but most of them will simply occur in Chloey's existing eight scenes.

Of course, who knows? I may do the rewrite and realize it sucks. That's kind of how the rewrite process is. You do your best to fix and tweak, and sometimes you get things wrong. However, in this case, I think this will work simply because I'm excited about it and it really ties in so perfectly with Eugene's work.

So when examining your supporting cast, do what I just did. Figure out what's missing from those characters' lives. What can you do to make them the stars of their own movies in their heads? Then think about how those changes will affect the rest of your script.

Scene Conflict Pass

Once you make sure each scene serves a purpose, then you need to focus on making it as strong as possible. This is honestly where the bulk of your rewriting will happen. It can take days or weeks or months to get everything right. The easiest way to do this is to remember that every scene needs conflict. So what is conflict? Generally speaking, it is opposing or competitive actions or struggles. In writing, it is the compelling material that drives your story forward. Conflict is integral to your story because, without it, you don't have a story. Without conflict all you have are characters who are nothing but happy and smile all the time. Who wants to read that?

The two main kinds of conflict are internal and external. There are different kinds of external conflict, and the kind you use really depends on what kind of story you are telling and where in the story you are. For example, if you are writing an action story, your conflict would be more physical. Maybe your hero wants to break into the terrorist fort and save the president, but the terrorist wants to keep the president prisoner. The conflict would become physical when the hero attacks and kills the terrorist.

But external conflict also can be more subtle. In a romantic comedy, it might be palpable tension between two characters who are mad at each other but aren't yet at the yelling stage.

Are you getting the picture? Here are a few more examples:

In a thriller, your main conflict may be a cop who wants to catch a serial killer, but of course the serial killer wants to keep killing. If you wrote a pitch (which, as you'll recall, I always recommend) you should already know your main character's want and the main antagonistic force that is getting in their way. That's good, but that one main conflict shouldn't be the only conflict in your story. Every scene needs conflict, and the easiest way to create it is by constantly raising the stakes.

What do I mean by raising the stakes? Well, recall that a

character normally has three important things in their life: their personal life (family and friends), their romantic life and their career. If you want to raise conflict, put all three in jeopardy.

Let's say you are writing a romantic comedy. Obviously in question will be your protagonist's love life, but a way to stir up trouble even further would be to also mess with their career and home life. Maybe as a result of the romantic drama, your protagonist is now in a fight with their best friend or another supporting cast member; or maybe because of a romantic choice they made, their job is now on the line.

Another way to drive a scene forward is to introduce internal conflict. This is conflict that exists inside of a character, such as struggling with a decision. In comic books and film, it's sometimes harder to show a character who is suffering from an internal struggle without making it overly obvious, but it's possible and important to the storytelling process.

Basically ask yourself, "What's the absolute worst thing that could go wrong?" That's what I mean by raising the stakes.

But even once you add conflict to your scene, you aren't done. Now you need to do everything you can to make that conflict stronger. For example, let's say the couple in your story is about to break up. Originally you made the breakup scene take place in their living room. How can you up the conflict? Making their breakup take place at Thanksgiving dinner with all the family watching would seriously up the conflict.

Or maybe you have a scene in which a guy gets fired from his office job? How can you add more conflict to that scene, since getting fired is already pretty big on its own? Well, you need to raise the stakes. If this guy is well off, does it really matter or hurt him that he's getting fired? But if this guy has a sick kid and medical bills up his wazoo, then getting fired would be devastating. Sometimes to raise conflict in a scene, you need to look at the scenes around it.

Another way to add conflict, particularly in Act III, is to add a ticking clock device. So think of a bomb that is about to explode. That ticking clock brings extra pressure. A good example of this is in Christmas movies. There is a ticking clock already built into the structure, because the basic plot is that your character(s) must save Christmas or it will be ruined. The calendar becomes the ticking clock.

There are lots of different kinds of conflict, and you need to make sure every scene has at least one. If it doesn't, then you need to do whatever is necessary to add it.

In "Virgin Dad," one of the scenes I'm really unhappy with is that first scene in which Eugene learns that Meta is his daughter. It's probably one of the worst-written scenes in my whole first draft. So before I sit down to rewrite it, I want to examine it.

The first thing I need to do is get rid of Ramirez. His character never shows up again and I didn't like him. The next issue is that the scene needs more conflict. Eugene wants to get to work because he is late for the big meeting with his boss. That means he is in a hurry, and anything else that comes up would be distracting. On the flip side we have Meta, and she wants Eugene to be her father. That should give us a lot of good conflict. So let's see:

```
INT. EUGENE'S APARTMENT BUILDING LOBBY -
MOMENTS LATER

The stairwell opens and Eugene flies out
```

of it, running into META, a 12-year-old girl with short blue hair. He falls to the floor.

Meta, unfazed, looks at him, more annoyed than anything else. She notices his security badge and ID for TimeBox Squared.

                META
     You're Eugene Baker?

Eugene stands and walks to the front door of the building.

               EUGENE
    No, I'm Dr. Eugene Baker, ScD.

He exits and Meta chases after him.

EXT. EUGENE'S APARTMENT - CONTINUOUS

Eugene turns, heading up the sidewalk and toward downtown Bethesda.

                META
      Hey, wait up!

               EUGENE
    I'm sorry, I don't have time for Girl Scouts. I'm late for an important meeting.

                META
    I'm not a Girl Scout.

               EUGENE
    Then who are you?

                META
    I'm Meta Baker-Alexander, your daughter.

Eugene stops in his tracks and looks back at her.

                      EUGENE
        I assure you, I don't have a
        daughter.

He then crosses the street, forcing Meta to dodge around a bicycle messenger.

                      META
        That's not true, 'cause here I
        am.

                      EUGENE
        I've never had relations with a
        woman, thus it is impossible for
        me to be your father.

EXT. DOWNTOWN BETHESDA - CONTINUOUS

Eugene crosses the street and enters downtown Bethesda. Meta is still chasing him.

                      META
        You think I'm happy about this?
        Look at you. You're like a time
        traveler from the 1950s.

                      EUGENE
        Says the vertically challenged
        hobbit with blue hair.

                      META
        That's part of my branding!

Eugene reaches the end of the block and stops at an empty intersection because the "don't walk" sign is flashing.

Meta keeps on walking but stops short when she realizes that Eugene is still waiting for the "walk" sign.

>   META
>   The New Haven Sperm Bank.

Eugene's eyes go wide.

>   META
>   My mom worked at the bank. She
>   used your junk and made herself
>   preggers.

>   EUGENE
>   That's illegal and unethical.

Meta pulls out a crumbled piece of paper.

>   META
>   If it makes you feel any better,
>   Mom felt so guilty that she put
>   you on the birth certificate.

The street sign shifts to "walk" and Eugene crosses the road, heading toward a subway entrance.

>   EUGENE
>   I don't have time for this. Have
>   your mother or your mother's
>   lawyer contact me.

>   META
>   Mom died last week. So either
>   you take me in or put me into
>   the system, though after meeting
>   you I'm not sure which is worse.

An alarm on Eugene's watch beeps. He's now 10 minutes late!

```
                        EUGENE
                Fine, come with me. We will sort
                this out later.

     The two enter the subway.
```

Is the scene perfect? No, but it's so much better than what I had. It went from being a five- to six-page scene to a two-page scene. In fact, if you compare the two scenes side by side, the beats are fairly close. The differences here are that I got rid of the extra character and the dialogue is a lot tighter because now that I've finished my first draft, I know Eugene's and Meta's voices. What I'm most happy about here is the vibe between the two characters. They have chemistry, which was missing in the original version.

When I rework this scene again, the first thing I'll do is cut Eugene bumping into her. I'm just not happy with that. It's also weird that she just shows up at his place, so I may move the whole scene somewhere else, but that's just how this goes. You rework a scene and rework a scene until it's finally a much stronger version than the original.

Dialogue Pass

Once we have locked in your scenes — once they each have strong conflict and serve the overall purpose of the story — then it's time to move on to dialogue. Go through and cut any piece that is small talk or other filler. Then go back in and tweak every piece so that each character has a unique voice and speech pattern. Another thing to do is to cut your first and last piece of dialogue from every scene (which you did some of already when we talked about the "enter late, leave early" rule).

Yup, you're waiting *all the way until now* to do your dialogue pass. Why? Because very few scenes from your original draft actually remain in the final draft. Had you edited your dialogue earlier, you would have spent countless hours perfecting scenes that aren't even around anymore. I don't know what you call that, but where I'm from that's called "wasting time." So you want to wait until your script is as solid as possible before doing a final dialogue pass. Plus, we tend not to really know our characters until we're almost finished with their story, so by now we have a much better feel for what they'd say or do, which should help make their dialogue more authentic and fun.

For me, the dialogue pass is one of the easier tasks in rewriting. I generally do it late in the process, when just about everything is locked down. I also do it character by character. For example, if I were doing a Meta dialogue pass, I would read each and every one of her scenes back to back, double checking every line of her dialogue. I'd make sure nothing sounds out of place and that everything is as concise as it should be. Once I did that, I might move on to Eugene or even Chloey.

Writing Pass

Once you've locked in your scenes — once you've spent hours upon hours fixing and tweaking them — it will be time to work over your action lines. Finally, it's time to do a cleanup. Start at the top of your script and do a read-through in which you tweak every sentence, making it clean and pretty. Now is the time to worry about grammar, making sure your action lines pop and all that jazz.

Beyond the obvious things, you really need to keep an eye out for something called "draft dust." Every time you make a change or tweak during the rewrite process, it can affect scenes that you don't even realize. Let's say in the first draft of your script your main character was wearing their favorite red shirt because later on you wanted a scene a in which someone makes fun of that shirt or something. When rewriting you realized it was silly and you cut the whole making-fun thing because it served no purpose. Well, then you also need to go back to Act I, where the shirt was first introduced, and cut it too, because now it also serves no purpose.

The more and more rewriting you do, the more you'll have scattered pieces of description throughout the whole thing or you may have a character refer to something that was cut. So a writing pass is really the only time you need to start at Page 1 and work all the way to the end, because you need to clear out all the draft dust and make sure all the prose flows and sounds pretty.

If you are dyslexic like me and this is something you have a problem with, then don't forget that you can always clean up as much as you can, and then turn the script over to a freelance editor who will find all those problem areas.

Assignment Time

Rewrite your script.

This is it. This is the big one. This is where you can spend months or years working and writing.

CHAPTER EIGHTEEN

Now What?

There often is a time in the screenwriting process when you will hit a wall. For most of us it happens several drafts in, and no matter how good or how experienced you are, it always happens. Writing and rewriting a screenplay takes hundreds of hours. That's a lot of time to be spending in not just your head, but also in the heads of all your characters and this crazy world you've built for them.

Hitting a wall means that, somewhere along the line, you got too close. You are no longer objective to the story or the storytelling. Being stuck in rewrites and passes for weeks can blind you to all the cool, fresh things about your story.

Do you remember when you wrote your pitch? How exciting and new it felt? Do you remember how much fun it was putting those first few words down on the page? That feeling will be gone.

With me, it normally happens around draft three or four. I'll be struggling with how to fix a problem with Act II, and I'll start to hate my characters. I'll start to hate the world. I'll think to myself, "Oh my god, I'm a hack. This is the worst thing anyone has ever written. I hate myself. I'm making a mistake. This is wrong!"

It's a horrible place to be as a writer, but it's OK because there are ways to combat it. In my case, I'm lucky because I talk to my editor. In fact, we've worked together for so many years that he knows when in the writing process to expect the phone call, and using a calm, reassuring voice he talks me down off the ledge.

A writer friend of mine does something really neat. When she's just started planning — so somewhere between writing a pitch and a treatment — she writes a letter to herself. She explains why she chose this story: why it matters and why it's important that she's the one to tell it. When she hits that wall in the rewrite process, she drops the letter in the mail. A few days later it shows up and it gives her enough strength to jump back in and get the rewrites done.

Another common approach is simply to walk away. If you are feeling frustrated, just walk away. Put the screenplay down for a month and come back with fresh eyes. That time away will help remind you what was so magical about the story to begin with. And just remember that this is a normal writing thing — whether your medium of choice is graphic novels, screenplays, stage plays or books, it happens to us all and you shouldn't let it get to you.

Once you do your cleanup, you will officially have a second draft! So then what? Normally that's when I send it to my readers. I also send a copy to a script consultant I know in L.A. (we went to school together), my publisher and my best friend. I have all three read it and, based on their feedback, I jump back in and start draft three. If you don't have people who are educated about writing and can give you real constructive feedback, then another option is to do nothing. Don't touch your story or think about it. Walk away and start something completely different. Maybe you spend a month or two writing a novella, or you start the planning process on a new script. Working on something different and coming back to it later will make all the difference.

Of course the big question, though, is how do you know when you are finished? The right answer is generally that you are never finished with a script until it's made into a movie. That's just how the business works, and it means that at the end of the day, you simply have to use your best judgment and know when it's finally time to move on to your next project for good.

It's important to keep looking ahead. Finishing your first screenplay is an amazing achievement, but it's only the beginning. The single best thing you can do instead of worrying about whether your screenplay is done is to start your next one. Look back at how much you've grown through the process of writing this first one, and think about how much more you will grow by writing your next!

If you do dream about moving to Hollywood and being a "real" screenwriter, you will need more than one screenplay in your portfolio. Plus, moving on to a new project will give you even more distance, so that when you come back and look at your first screenplay again, you'll be able to recognize many more of its problems.

Assignment Time

Send your script out to some trusted educated people for them to read. Then take their notes and continue on with the rewriting process. Good luck!

About the Author

Scott King was born in Washington D.C. and raised in Ocean City, Maryland. He received his undergraduate degree in film from Towson University, and his M.F.A. in film from American University. He currently teaches at the University of Maryland Eastern Shore.

"DAD! A Documentary Graphic Novel," King's first book, was published in Fall '09. He is also the creator and writer of "Holiday Wars."

To learn more about King and his work visit his website at www.scottking.info. You can also follow him on twitter via @ScottKing.

Made in United States
North Haven, CT
22 August 2024